FROM RUCKSACK
TO BACKPACK

From Rucksack to Backpack

A Young Woman's Journey in a Newly Evolving World

Juliane Heyman

To order additional copies of this book, contact:
Xlibris Corporation
1-888-795-4274
www.Xlibris.com
Orders@Xlibris.com
22459

"Compelling, Inspirational, Pioneering. Juliane Heyman's life and travels are all of these things and more. She is a woman before her time, and her stories capture an era when travel was truly an adventure and an education. A book for every woman who dreams of seeing the world, and making a difference in it."

-AMIEE WHITE BEAZLEY, *Aspen Daily News*

"This fascinating book offers glimpses of an extraordinary life: that of a woman whose questing spirit led her from a childhood fleeing the Nazis during World War II to an adventurous adulthood traveling and working as one of the first Americans (and often the only Western female) in remote areas of post-colonial Asia (including Vietnam, India, Pakistan and Afghanistan in the 1950s.) The author provides an eyewitness account of rapid historical change and a vivid portrait of cultures and terrains in distant lands."

-Rebecca Larson, Author, *Daughters of Light*

"It is distinct pleasure to join Juliane Heyman on her travels to faraway lands when college-age travelers were few and never on their own. The author's curiosity about people makes her stays in such places as Vietnam and Afghanistan in the 1950s fascinating reading; this book belongs in every traveler's library and has special relevance today."

-Nick DeWolf, Photographer and Inventor

CONTENTS

ACKNOWLEDGMENTS

My heartfelt thanks to all those who offered me their support and encouragement. Numerous participants in the Aspen Writers' Foundation Weekly Writers' Group have read parts of the book and given me valuable criticism, particularly the moderator, Amiee White Beazley of the Aspen Daily News.

I wish to give special tribute to two friends, Maggie DeWolf and Ruth Glater who encouraged me and made important suggestions. Amanda Dworski and Lisa Skelton have provided editorial assistance.

INTRODUCTION

I was born on the Baltic in the Free City of Danzig, now Gdansk, Poland, in 1925. From the 12th century until the middle of the 15th century, Danzig remained an independent city state. For the next 500 years it was under Polish rule. From 1793 until 1918, Danzig was governed by the Germans. In 1918 the allies who defeated Germany decreed that the city and its surrounding territory, about 730 square miles in all, would be independent of both Germany and Poland.

My childhood in Europe had an important influence on my later life, because I survived the Second World War and was extremely fortunate to have escaped the Nazis. My luck was always with me and I felt I was invulnerable.

My parents had moved to Danzig after the first World War. They were in business together importing and exporting grain all over Europe. My mother, who had a Ph.D in law from the University of Wuerzburg, Germany, was born in Duesseldorf. My father had come from a small town, Zempelburg, in Eastern Germany, now Sepolno, Poland.

The business had become very successful by the early 1920's. The family was quite well off financially, and lived in an affluent neighborhood.

The first eight years of my childhood were very

happy. I played in our beautiful garden with my brother who was a year and a half older. Since both my parents were at work all day, we were alone and became quite independent and self-sufficient. However, the family spent weekends together. In summer we went to the beach to swim and from an early age I was a good swimmer. I loved my parents and learned much from them whenever we were together.

I began attending a German-speaking school in 1931. The first two years were very pleasant until 1933 when the Nazis had come to power and things changed. Children were told not to play with me during recess. There were no other Jewish children in the school and I had to be by myself. At about the same time, my best friend, the blond daughter of a chauffeur in the neighborhood, was ordered not to play with me. Needless to say, I found these ostracisms most upsetting.

In 1935 when Jewish children were no longer permitted to attend public school, I transferred to a newly established Jewish school. I liked the school and had many friends, but the ten-minute walk to and from it each day made me very apprehensive. The Nazi boys harassed me and sometimes even hit me. My mother tried to console me, but could not protect me.

In 1938 the Nazis imprisoned my parents for a few days for some unknown reason, but mainly because they were Jewish. During these days I was devastated and lonely, particularly since my brother was in school in England. Several months after their release from prison, they heard that the authorities were going to come again and we decided to leave immediately.

It was a very traumatic experience for me to depart in the middle of the night, leaving everything that was dear to me, my school, my friends, the house, the garden and our loyal help. I sensed that I would never return. I tried not to cry, as I did not want to upset Mother and Father. I realized that I should not interfere with all the grown-ups around the house. We crossed the border to Gdynia, Poland, thus beginning an 18 month odyssey.

My parents stayed in Gdynia to liquidate the business. I was sent to a school in Switzerland. I traveled by myself via Germany, and at the border was subjected to a strip-search by the Germans. I don't know what they were looking for, perhaps jewelry or cash, but I was very upset and scared. To my great relief they let me continue.

After a term at the Swiss school, I joined my parents in Brussels, Belgium, where they had started a new life which meant I had to adapt to a new school system and a new language. I studied most of the time. My only recreation was participating in the activities of the Girl Scouts on the weekends.

When the Germans invaded Poland in September 1939, we realized how fortunate we were having left Danzig, which was the first town the Germans occupied. My brother, who was on vacation with us, did not return to England, since my parents decided it was safer to be in neutral Belgium than in war-torn England.

On May 10, 1940, we heard the sound of gunfire outside our Brussels apartment. It was totally unexpected. We went to the balcony, and within a short time, realized that the Germans had invaded Belgium.

After a few days we left by train and headed to the

coast. The trip took ten hours instead of the normal two. From there we crossed the French border on foot with our rucksacks on our backs. We then hitched a ride on a horse-drawn wagon and arrived in Dunkirk, where we spent three days in a cellar which had become a shelter. It was the time of the British evacuation from the continent, which we did not know at the time.

The family continued, with no idea where we were going. As we walked along the road, we repeatedly were caught in the crossfire between French and German forces. One day I was lying in a ditch and the man next to me lost a leg in the fire. How lucky I was, that nothing happened to me or my family.

For the next two weeks we worked in a bakery in Abbeville for a French woman who took us in. German soldiers frequently came to the shop and commandeered some bread. Once, as my brother and I ran an errand for the bakery, some soldiers stopped to ask us if we were Jewish. By pretending not to understand German, my brother fended them off, while I tried to be calm. One soldier pointed his gun at us, threatening to kill us. Another soldier who had joined the group said: "Let them go, they are French."

During the battle of the Somme all inhabitants had to evacuate the town. We joined the family of our kind host and moved to the village Noyelles-en-Chaussez, where we spent several weeks working on a farm. I learned how to milk cows and did other tasks. When the owners of the farm returned from their flight after the armistice we got a ride on a truck to Paris, where I had an aunt. However, she had fled. My brother and I had to stand in line for hours for food for the family.

Eventually my parents obtained some false documents to enter the unoccupied zone of France. At the border the train was stopped, but the German authorities did not discover that the papers were forged. To my great relief we had escaped from the Nazis again.

We spent several months on a farm near Bordeaux in the wine country. My father was a co-owner of the winery, together with his cousins who lived there. I learned to make wine, which I enjoyed. Mother and Father often went to Marseilles to the American Consulate and finally succeeded in receiving visas for the U.S. Our Danzig passports had helped. Citizens of Germany and Poland had to wait much longer, as the U.S. quotas for those countries were over-subscribed. Many, including most of my relatives did not make it and were killed in the concentration camps. We did not learn of this till the end of the war.

Lisbon, Portugal was the only port in Western Europe from which ships could sail to the U.S. This meant we had to cross Spain, which did not give us visas. Therefore we walked illegally over the Pyrenees with a guide. Since it was night and we were not allowed to talk, I remember little of the trip. At the Spanish border we took a third-class train through Spain and arrived in Lisbon a few days later. I experienced a tremendous sense of relief. While waiting for the freighter for America, I felt free and secure in Portugal and gorged myself on food, which I had not been able to do for over a year.

When our boat passed the Statue of Liberty in New

York, cliché or not, it was and remains to this day the symbol of our family's deliverance. I was moved beyond words and looked forward to a new life in the United States without the dangers of the past. I tried not to think of the childhood years, and hardly ever mentioned it to anyone for many years. Only the tragedy of what had happened to our relatives brought tremendous pain to my family.

I had not been in school for a year and a half. My parents sent me first to a boarding school to learn English where I experienced culture shock, since the high school girls were so different from me. I hardly knew what they were talking about. Then I spent a semester at home in our apartment in New York, while attending a special school to learn American literature and history, which I had never studied.

In February 1943 I was admitted to Barnard College of Columbia University. I had adjusted to life in America and my college years were normal and pleasant, like those of my fellow students. I graduated in 1946 with a degree in International Relations.

The first story in these memoirs is one that took place during the war, while I was at Barnard. The others start in 1951. By that time I had received two Masters degrees from the University of California Berkeley, one in International Relations and one in Library Science. In 1949 I was accepted to a special intern program at the Library of Congress in Washington where I worked for over a year in the Legislative Reference Service doing research for Congress. It was a fascinating experience and I learned a great deal about politics.

At a meeting for the interns, Luther Evans, the Librarian of Congress said: "Some of you will have a career in the Library of Congress, while others will go out into the world."

I chose to go out into the world, and got a job as a civilian librarian for the Air Force in Japan where I had a chance to see a great deal of the country, as I was stationed in three different regions. It was the beginning of life in other countries.

When I finished my work in Japan I was determined to see more of the world. The second story is the beginning of that journey.

RUCKSACK

It was during World War II that I attended Barnard College in New York City. My parents had moved to California and I was living in the dormitories.

One of my best friends was Lisbet, a Swedish girl married to an American GI who was overseas. She was the only married woman in college and had a small apartment not far from Barnard.

During one college holiday, we decided to leave New York City and go for a hike in the country. Lisbet showed me a map of Pennsylvania.

"This looks like an interesting area," she said pointing to the Poconos mountains. Neither one of us had ever been to Pennsylvania, which was not too far. We planned to spend a couple days surrounded by nature.

Lisbet prepared a few sandwiches, and I bought fruit and cookies. We each packed a toothbrush, a change of underwear, socks, sweater and a clean shirt into small rucksacks. We did not take water, as at that time you could drink the water of the streams.

We went to the bus station in the Spring of 1943 and bought tickets to a small village in the Poconos. After a few hours' bus trip, we arrived in the countryside and began to hike on part of the Appalachian trail system. We traveled through woodlands, lakes, ponds and rivers.

Lovely wildflowers, many unfamiliar to us, covered the rolling mountains. We enjoyed the beautiful landscape and the silence as there were hardly any other persons on the trail. The trail did not seem difficult, since we both had hiked in Europe on more strenuous terrain.

In the afternoon we returned to the trailhead. Soon the bus came and took us to the town of Wilkesbar, which we had found on the map. Since it was not common to camp and we had no camping equipment, we planned to find a cheap, clean room for the night.

Once in Wilkesbar, with our rucksacks on our backs, we found there were no signs indicating a room in a home or small hotel in that part of town. Though tired and looking forward to a shower, we assumed that the right place would be found and continued searching.

All of a sudden a police car stopped next to us containing two police officers. "Get in!" shouted one of the two harshly. We hesitated. Why should we get into the police car? I was perplexed. One officer opened the car's door, stepped out and repeated in a commanding voice, "Get in."

We still hesitated. He then pushed us into the car. I didn't know whether to laugh or cry and asked him, "What have we done?"

"We are taking you to the police station for some questioning," he said, a little less harshly than previously. I could not understand why, and wondered what was going to happen.

Within a few minutes we arrived at the police station and were ordered to walk up the stairs, followed by the same officer.

"Well, well, what are you bringing us here?" said the police captain of the station in the interrogation room. He was a middle-aged man in a-well fitting uniform and did not seem mean to me, like a Nazi in Europe. For both of us it was our first experience with the police in the United States.

Turning to us he proceeded to ask for our names, addresses, occupation, age and other personal data.

"Why are you in Wilkesbar?" he wanted to know.

"We have been hiking in the Poconos and were looking for a room to spend the night," said Lisbet.

He could not understand—or didn't want to believe—that we had been hiking, since hiking only became popular in the United States after the war.

When he learned that Lisbet was Swedish and married to an American soldier, he asked, "Does your husband know you are here?"

"How could he? He is stationed somewhere in Europe, and I don't even know where he is and am unable to communicate with him."

The captain learned from me that I was a foreign student and that my parents lived in California.

"Do your parents know that you are here?"

I could truthfully answer "yes" as it was my mother's birthday and I had called her collect from the bus station.

The interrogation continued for a while, and gradually the captain realized that we were honest but naïve college students who had not realized we were walking in a red light district. He explained that having knapsacks on our backs was suspicious. It looked like we were run-away girls heading towards prostitution. The lesson I learned was not to walk with a rucksack or daypack in a city. Only years later did they become a common sight in American cities.

He asked the two officers who had picked us up to take us to a respectable boarding house. The two politely opened the car doors for us and drove for about 20 minutes. During the entire trip they were cordial and pleasant and talked about the city.

"This lady has rooms and it is a good place for you," said the officer when we arrived at a small modest house in a neighborhood of other similar houses. "The landlady will take good care of you."

Obviously we didn't dare to look for any other accommodations and were happy that our arrest ended this way. The landlady was a plumb, pleasant woman dressed in a simple housecoat. She showed us a room with two beds, a chair and a table. The bathroom was down the hall, everything was clean and the price seemed reasonable.

We slept well after a simple dinner she offered us for a little extra money. The next morning we took public transportation to the main bus station heading back to New York City. We decided we didn't want to continue hiking after the previous night's adventure.

INDIA
1951-1952

CHINESE GOODWILL MISSION TO INDIA

"I am not going with you around the world, as I decided to go to graduate school," wrote Ruth. I received this disappointing letter from my friend the summer of 1951. We were both working as civilians for the U.S. Air Force in Japan but in different cities. We had been friends ever since we met on a troopship from California to Japan, where in our free time we explored.

Ruth and I got along well, and we decided to save as much money as we could in order to journey home via the long route, instead of returning directly to the United States. Now she had changed her plans. I was upset but understood her reasons. I had been dreaming and planning to go slowly around the world, making a stop in India where I had an Indian friend from graduate school at the University of California at Berkeley. Should I give up my dreams and plans just because my friend was not coming along? After much thought, debating the pros and cons, I decided to travel alone. After all, the money I had saved in Japan was for the trip.

It was not common at that time for a twenty-six year-old woman to travel alone. My parents in California and some friends were not happy with my decision. I didn't care; I was going to do this with or without anyone else.

I began to plan my trip. There were some freighters going to India from Japan. These freighters allowed passengers, and they were cheaper than other modes of transportation. Besides, I reasoned, freighters stopped at various places to load or unload their cargo, which gave me a chance to visit many places without having hotel expenses.

The *Sangola*, a British ship that was leaving for India shortly after I finished my tour with the Air Force, seemed just right for my plans. I packed two small suitcases with summer clothes and some rain gear while the Air Force sent my other possessions to my parents in California.

When the ship left Japan, it had only three passengers: Peggy, a British lady who lived in Rangoon, Burma (now Myamar), Mr. White, a tall and friendly Englishman who had to go to Calcutta on some business, and me, the only American.

The first stop of the *Sangola* was Hong Kong. The three of us went sightseeing for two or three days while the ship picked up some freight. We took the Peak Tram to Victoria Peak with its magnificent vistas of the surrounding mountains, the city below and the busy harbor. A visit to Aberdeen, which was packed solid with fishing boats, included a delicious meal at one of those floating restaurants. We took tea in the famous Peninsula Hotel with its ornate lobby, where the British Governor surrendered to the Japanese in World War II. In downtown Hong I was amazed to see so many shops with jewelry, silk, handicrafts and other items, all of which were extremely cheap at the time. We also visited numerous temples and pagodas in addition to the bustling Chinese Market with various live animals and fresh vegetables.

When we returned for the departure, we learned that twenty-four Chinese, on an official goodwill mission to India, were going to be our fellow passengers.

I was intrigued and wanted to know more about these travelers, particularly since I had nothing important to do during the twenty-day journey to Calcutta. This was the first goodwill mission from China to India. The men and women spoke English well; one young woman had an American accent. Dressed in stylish Western clothes, they looked prosperous. They carried the latest models of typewriters and other consumer gadgets. This was very surprising, as we knew about the poverty in China and Mao's emphasis on equalitarianism.

The Chinese never talked to us even to say "good morning" when we passed them on the deck. The officers didn't seem to have any relations with them either.

They huddled together, occupying all the deck chairs, talking loudly, sometimes in English, other times in Chinese. We did not exist for them as they took over the bar as well as the little writing room.

I felt that they were spying on us, as they constantly tried to look into the cabins of Western passengers. It was not the custom on freighters to lock one's cabin but theirs were always locked and the curtains drawn. They didn't eat with us, and had their meals at a special sitting.

We ate with the British officers and Robin Bannerjee, the ship's Indian doctor, of the *Sangola* becoming a close family that often made fun of the Chinese. However, the captain warned us to be careful. He reminded us we were traveling on a British ship. Britain, unlike the United States, had recognized China in 1950, one year after the establishment of the Republic of China.

I decided to learn as much as I could about the goodwill mission. I tried to sit as close as possible in order to listen to their conversation, frequently in English. The discussion I overheard dealt with educational reform. One man spoke seven languages. They were supposed to represent the people of China, but why did they travel first class, eat European food and wear Western clothes? That is not what I expected from communists. I had a distorted and unreal idea about communists formed to some extent by having lived in Washington during the McCarthy years. To my knowledge, I had never met or seen any communists in the United States or Japan.

Like most Americans at the time, I had been conditioned to hate communists. In the 1940s and 1950s the House Committee on Un-American Activities conducted widely publicized anti-communist investigations, often referred to as "witch-hunts" because they used reckless and unfair tactics. We were supposed to be afraid of communists. I was very much opposed to the hearings that were held to investigate the influence of communists, particularly in the film industry. The result was the imprisonment of a group of writers, directors and producers known as the Hollywood Ten. Now I was meeting communists who did not fit the image that Senator McCarthy tried to convey.

As scheduled, the *Sangola's* next stop after Hong Kong was Singapore. Before the freighter could dock, immigration and health officials came aboard to clear all the passengers. (Singapore, as part of Malaya, was still a British colony at that time.) The Chinese claimed they had diplomatic immunity and refused to see the British officials. The authorities insisted and would not let the freighter dock unless all passengers followed the procedure. The alternative would have been to return to Hong Kong without having unloaded the freight.

The captain was outraged. A lot of commotion followed. There were loud arguments between the leader of the Chinese group and the captain. Later, the captain told us that he would have liked to put the Chinese under quarantine, so that they would have to leave the ship. However, that would have upset the British Colonial Office.

After a delay of four hours, very costly to the freighter, the captain had finally persuaded the Chinese to be cleared, so that we could unload the ship. Peggy, Mr. White and I—as well as the officers—were delighted and considered it a victory for the British. The three of us disembarked to visit Singapore while our Chinese companions had to stay on board guarded by the British Police of Singapore. That evening we celebrated our victory by taking over the bar. For once, the Chinese did not show up.

The next stop was Penang, in Malaya (now Malaysia). The communist guerrillas who had fought the Japanese occupation during World War II had begun an armed struggle to take over the country. These guerillas were largely recruited from the Chinese population. The British had declared a state of emergency that lasted from 1948 to 1960. *Sangola's* captain prohibited the Chinese passengers to leave the boat, because of their behavior in Singapore.

Peggy, Robin and I left to sightsee. On the second day we took a long hike in the hills surrounding Penang. It was a dense jungle. Only a narrow path lead us through this lush rainforest containing the most beautiful, exotic and colorful plants that I had ever seen. The particular variety of trees there was very tall and seemed to touch the sky. It was hot and humid. There were clouds hanging over the hills which gave it a mystical feeling.

Suddenly we saw a man walking alone in the forest. We thought we recognized him as one of the goodwill mission passengers. We were puzzled, but continued our hike.

When we returned to the *Sangola* we were confronted by two British intelligence officers who questioned us about our trip. They explained that a Chinese/Malayan guerrilla had been caught in the same area where we had been. They believed that one of the Chinese had illegally left the freighter to contact the guerrillas in Penang. I told them that I thought we had seen one of the passengers in the jungle, though I was not sure. Apparently, there was not enough proof, and as far as I could tell, all passengers were with us all the way to India. I certainly had not been aware that there was a danger while we were hiking, but I was glad to be back safely aboard the ship.

The last stop before arriving in Calcutta was Rangoon, the capital of Burma, which had become independent in 1948. The town's infrastructure had been shattered, and many buildings were in disrepair. The communists had spread through the country in the 1950s, yet it seemed that the Burmese were unconcerned with the violence around them. I found them very hospitable. Peggy left the *Sangola* and invited Robin and me to her house. I believe the Chinese also visited the town, since the British had no authority over their action in this independent country.

Without any further incident and with an Indian delegation at the dock to welcome the goodwill mission, I disembarked in Calcutta along with the Chinese.

AN INDIAN WEDDING

"You must come to my wedding," wrote Satya Agarwal, "The wedding party passes through New Delhi on December 12, and I will meet you at the station."

I had known Satya while we were graduate students at the University of California, Berkeley, two years earlier. A mutual friend in India had told him that I had arrived in India six weeks before.

I went to the station with only my toothbrush. I packed no extra clothes, since I had no idea what I was getting into, nor how long this wedding would last. I had never been to an Indian wedding and was not familiar with the customs and ceremonies. It was thrilling to have the privilege to participate in such an important event of a friend.

At the appointed hour the train from Bikaner arrived at the railroad station, which was noisy and crowded with Indians in different outfits accompanied by many boxes and assorted luggage. Satya found me immediately, as I was the only Western woman in a skirt and blouse. "I am so happy that you are here. You must honor me with your presence at my wedding. Please join our wedding party," he said.

As is common in India, it was an arranged marriage. Satya had met Urmila, his future bride, only once during the engagement party a few months prior.

We had a few refreshments at the buffet, then boarded the train for the bride's hometown of Muzafarnagar, about four hours from Delhi. When the train was ready to leave, Satya and I entered the compartment of the "Wedding Party." In the compartment were only men. Male members of the bridegroom's family went to the wedding, while the women, including the mother and sisters, stayed home. Some of the men were wearing Western clothes; some were in the Indian dhoti. Satya introduced me to his father, four brothers and a number of cousins, uncles, nephews and friends. There were about thirty men when the train departed Delhi. At almost every stop between Delhi and our destination more friends and distant relatives joined the group. When we arrived at Muzafarnagar, I was the only woman in a party of about forty-four men.

We were traveling in third-class, the cheapest and most uncomfortable railroad class. Usually third-class compartments are overcrowded and one rarely finds a seat. I was surprised at these arrangements, because Satya had received a Ph.D at Berkeley and had a very important government position. Further, all his brothers, uncles and other male relatives were lawyers, doctors, professors or civil servants. It seemed to me they could at least afford a second-class compartment. Eventually I learned that the bridegroom had to pay the fare and expenses for everybody in the party. Since the group had its own compartment, it was not as bad as other third-class compartments, in which I had traveled previously.

At first I was uneasy and felt very uncomfortable among all those men.

"I don't know how to thank you for inviting me," I said to Satya trying to hide my discomfort.

He, as well as the others, tried hard to make me feel welcome, constantly expressing their pleasure at my presence. Only three years after independence from Britain, there were few Americans in India. To have a visitor from so far away seemed special to them, and it didn't matter that I was female.

The scenery that I viewed from the train was lovely. It was a fertile part of India. We passed lots of sugar cane fields and occasionally some factories. Many people were working in the fields. In the late afternoon, we arrived in Muzafarnagar, a small provincial town which was the center of sugar production in that northern Indian region.

About a dozen men from the bride's family, some with children, came to greet us with garlands of flowers. They placed the garlands around our necks. As we walked along, the town's band, in full dress uniform, accompanied us with music. I had to walk with Satya in front of the party and was very embarrassed to get so much attention. I almost felt like I was the bride. Satya's smile and pleasure reassured me that everybody was delighted with my presence. The men were then taken to various homes of the bride's family and friends.

I was taken to the large but sparsely furnished home of a prominent lawyer. The bathroom did not have plumbing, and the room I occupied had only a cot, a table and some chairs. My host was running for office for the Congress Party (the ruling party of India, the party of Prime Minister Nehru) in the forthcoming election. I never figured out his relationship to the bride. He and his sons made me feel very much at home. Indians are some of the most hospitable people, throughout my stay in India, I was always received with great hospitality.

I met some women from the house. At last I had a chance to be with the women and could talk to them. Most of them could converse in English. They were all related to Urmila, the bride. They insisted that I wear a sari, which I gladly did, since I had not brought one with me. They gave me a beautiful white one to wear. Then I accompanied these women to the bride's house, where all the ladies were dressed in the most exquisite saris in bright red, orange and purple, many embroidered with gold and silver. I couldn't take my eyes off the gorgeous colorful sight.

The bride's house was decorated with flowers and ribbons. In the middle of the patio was a canopy decorated with lights and artificial flowers.

Three hundred people had assembled, and the bride appeared. She was covered with many saris of different colors, veils and shawls. Only a tiny bit of her face was visible. With the help of some relatives she sat down in the middle of the patio surrounded by many ladies. She then received her gifts, primarily jewelry such as rings, bracelets, necklaces, earrings and jewelry for the forehead, the ankles and the nose. Everything was gold, silver or precious stones.

After an hour or so, the bridegroom arrived and Urmila put her garland around his neck. It was only the second time that they had seen each other. The women were chanting. Urmila's sister carried a tray with small lights to the bridegroom, which signified that she received him.

Now it was time for the most important part of the ceremony. In the large hall next to the patio, Satya received the men of his family and those of the bride's family. He then told one of the men to ask me to come to the hall. Again, I was treated more like a man. Even at this important moment, he wanted to make sure that I was comfortable.

Then everybody went to the center of the carpeted hall for the actual wedding ceremony. Somebody tried to get me a chair, though everybody else sat on the floor. I refused and sat with the men. When the bridegroom was in the center under the canopy, two Brahmin priests arrived. They read from the Veda in Sanskrit for about two hours. Afterwards, the couple was joined by knots in their clothing and they walked six times around the square under the canopy. Three times the bride followed the husband and three times the bride went ahead of the husband.

The bridal couple performed the prayers and walked around an open fire, which is most sacred to Hindus. While the priests were reading, the couple kept feeding the fire. A Hindu marriage, which is usually arranged, is not considered a contract, but something sacred, indissolvable in this life and in the hereafter.

During the entire ceremony Urmila never looked up, never smiled and only repeated modestly and quietly the words of the Brahmin priests. She was serene, while the guests in the room were moving around, talking with each other and having a good time.

A little game followed. The young couple had ribbons with seven knots around their wrists. In front of a candle, they had to untie the knots with the free hand. Satya finished first and therefore was the winner. The children in the room were delighted, laughing and screaming as they watched this exercise.

Late in the evening, we moved to long tables in the veranda for an elaborate meal. The many dishes included different curries, stews, rice, dahl, samosas, yogurt chapatis and many sweets. The host, Urmila's father, practically forced me to eat more than I wanted. He felt, as most Indians do, that if one does not encourage the guest to eat a lot, one is not a good host. The wedding day ended with pictures being taken, and afterwards I returned to the house of my host for much needed sleep.

I was asked by many to stay a few more days for more parties and wedding ceremonies, but I had to return to Delhi. I boarded the train exhausted but exhilarated by this unique experience.

INDIAN ELECTIONS

While I was a guest of one of the bride's relatives during the wedding in Muzafarnagar in 1951, I had the opportunity to meet several candidates for the first Indian election, which was going to take place the following year We chatted about the differences between Indian and American political campaigns.

"Why don't you stay a few more days after the wedding and accompany us to some villages where we will campaign?" said Mr. Hari Mohan, the son of a Congress Party candidate for the State Assembly. He was a tall man dressed in a light beige suit with a pleasant smile and twinkling dark eyes. The Congress Party was in power; it was the party of Nehru.

I was somewhat surprised, because I learned that Mr. Sham Lal, my host, was running for Parliament on the "Jan Sangh" ticket of the opposition party, a conservative party that attacked the government, corruption and the inefficiency and dishonesty of many officials but did not itself have a positive program. Candidates promised lower taxes, free education and other programs but had no answers on how to do it. Furthermore, the party wanted a reunion with Pakistan in a secular state but under Hindu domination. (Pakistan and India had both become independent states in 1948.) Though belonging to different parties, the two men were good friends.

"We will go with the Jan Sangh candidate to the country so that you get to see some Indian villages," said Hari. "Of course, I will accompany you."

"I am sorry, but I have to go back to Delhi now. However, I would love to take you up on your offer next week," I answered.

A week later I went back to Muzafarnagar. On a Friday afternoon we started out to the villages. Hari Mohan, Sham Lal, two of his assistants, a driver and I piled into an old Model-A Ford. Hari was in Western attire while Mr. Lal, a short dark-skinned man in his early 50s, was wearing the Indian dhoti, the white cotton outfit that Mahatma Gandhi always wore.

After about an hour driving on an unpaved, dusty road we turned from this main road to a path. In my opinion, this path was not meant for cars. It was very narrow and muddy with deep grooves. It didn't take long before we got stuck in the mud. All the men then got out of the car and pushed and pulled for half an hour. Somehow we got the Ford rolling again.

Finally we arrived in the village. While Sham Lal was busy canvassing, Hari and I walked around. It was my first exposure to Indian village life.

"This village, like most in this northern part of India, is more prosperous and has better facilities than most other villages in the country," said my companion.

All the houses were mud houses, each consisting of one room where an entire family—sometimes up to ten members—lived. Everything took place in this room. It contained only a few cots, occasionally a chair, but no table, closet or any other furniture. In one house a teenage boy studied by candlelight in a dark room. There was no electricity in the village and no sanitary facilities. The village women had to walk more than two miles for water from a well.

A man was smoking in the dark room in one house we visited. In another, women were cooking over an open fire in the middle of the room. The smoke was intense. In spite of this extreme poverty, the homes were rather clean. To me it seemed that this village was cleaner than some of the large cities that I had known like Delhi, Calcutta and Bombay.

What impressed me most was the warm hospitality that was extended to me, a foreigner, regardless of the poverty. Of course, the residents of the village were suspicious of foreigners, as they could not distinguish between Americans, or indeed any Westerners, and the British, their former colonial masters whom they disliked intensely at this time. Most were ignorant of the world outside India, and the only outsiders they knew were British.

Whenever we entered a house, I had to sit down, drink tea and eat sweets or other food that I was not familiar with. Sometimes I was reluctant, because I couldn't eat that much, but I realized that not accepting their food would have been an insult. I learned that hospitality is a very important part of Indian culture.

Later Mr. Lal told me that people had constantly asked him, "Who is this foreign lady in your group? Is your Jan Sangh Party financed by the British?"

"She is an American journalist who has come from far away and has nothing to do with my party," he would answer.

The village people, particularly the children, came

out to watch me. Their faces betrayed kindness, honesty and innocence. The children all paid respect to me by bowing and giving me the Indian greeting "namasteh."

In spite of their poverty, I had the impression that they were fairly content. They were not aware of a better life, as television portraying a different world was not yet available.

Some villagers had sugar cane fields. I had the opportunity to watch the entire process of how sugar is extracted from the cane without machinery. Two oxen went around and around a press, which extracted the juice from the cane. Everything else was processed by the men.

Among the many people I met in the village of about 2,000 inhabitants were the village elders. Most did not speak English, and not being able to converse with them frustrated me very much. Finally, I met a boy, perhaps 17 years old, who was studying for a college degree in Muzafarnagar, the nearest city. He was happy to practice his English with me and translated what the elders said. Mostly they welcomed me with polite phrases.

The only concrete building in the village was a school, established less than three years prior in 1949. The girls' school was not a concrete building; women were considered second-class citizens. Credit for this emphasis on education in this far-removed village went to the Congress Party. It was expected that most people were going to vote for the Congress Party. On the other hand, many people were supporting Mr. Lal, the Jan Sangh candidate, mainly for personal reasons. They liked him and believed his rhetoric.

When the women saw me, they ran away. They were afraid of foreigners. I noticed that women did not participate in any of the activities that took place that day in the village. When the children entertained us with songs in the village square, no women were present. Mr. Lal had arranged this event for the "honored guest," as he introduced me.

The next day I found myself in the company of Mr Lal in two small towns. He made very lengthy speeches that I did not understand. I always had to sit next to the candidate and often received garlands around my neck, as did he. It was not easy sitting demurely for hours at a time, while listening to these incomprehensible speeches.

People were curious about me, and it appeared that it was I that attracted the crowds. I was very much embarrassed. Hari told me that Mr. Lal had said, "This lady here has come from very far to observe the elections." People in the crowd whispered, according to my translator, "We are honored that a lady has come from so far." Other comments were: "These foreign women travel all over the world without their husbands and our wives cannot even go to the city two miles away."

In the second little town, the candidate said in my presence at a meeting: "Nehru has attacked Jan Sangh so strongly, that the party's name had become known in foreign countries and therefore this lady next to me has come to see for herself what is Jan Sangh."

Now I realized that the crowds might not have perceived me as an impartial observer. I had learned a great deal about Indian village life and elections. I did not want to be associated with this party, for which I had no sympathies. I did not want people to think that the United States was supporting Jan Sangh. I could not continue with this campaign in which I was being used by the candidate. I was upset and decided to return to Muzafarnagar.

In the election a few weeks later, the Congress Party won overwhelmingly. I came to learn that the candidates in India had to cope with many difficulties, such as poor roads, and had to finance their campaigns in such a way that only the well-to-do could enter a race. Four years after Independence, I had seen democracy at work.

THE GODDESS IN HARDWAR

Grace, her young student friend Satyapal and I decided to make a trip to Hardwar, to visit a woman who claimed to be the reincarnation of the goddess of Kashmir. Grace, an anthropologist and among the first group of Fulbright scholars in India, had heard about this goddess. I was anxious to accompany her and Satyapal.

We took the bouncing, crowded bus from Delhi for about six hours on dusty roads through northern Indian villages. Tired and dirty we arrived in Hardwar, one of India's holiest cities located where the Ganges emerged from the Himalaya to begin its slow progress across the plains. It was and still is a favored place for tens of thousands of Hindu pilgrims. I was anxious to learn why a person could become sacred and have so many followers.

The little town with many temples lay in the foothills where quiet forest groves of pines and firs nestled along rushing mountain streams. I was thrilled to be close to the mountains, which I had missed in the flat and desolate scenery of Delhi. Stone wall huts covered with roofs of bark and birch tree branches were scattered along the streets of Hardwar.

We arrived during the time of the evening prayer so we immediately proceeded to a room in the large building where the goddess was supposed to hold court. A huge mob was there as well as in the surrounding courtyard. Old men were chanting songs. Women in colorful cotton saris were holding crying babies.

Children of all ages in colorful, but not very clean outfits were running aimlessly around, adding to the confusion of the scene. Amid all this, I suddenly saw her.

She was a swarthy old woman sitting on the floor. Her dry face was deeply wrinkled and her mouth tightly closed. She was wearing a fiery red sari which covered her entire body and part of her face. Her head started to turn in circles to the rhythm of the drums and the chants of her disciples; first slowly, then faster and faster. Eventually, the movements of her head and arms were extremely violent. A portion of the sari fell off her head. Her long gray hair was hanging over her face as she passionately swung her entire body. This went on for several hours. She did not get tired. The show of incredible energy was apparently what attracted her many followers. I looked at the people, trying to see an expression of veneration which was not present.

Satyapal's sister, a disciple of the goddess, saw to it that food was served for us. I was not used to eating Indian food after witnessing how it was prepared. Sabzi (vegetables),dhal (curried lentil gravy) and rice were cooked in the courtyard right in front of us. Dirt from the floor was mixed in the dingy pots and the spicy, smoky smell did not add to the appeal of the meal. Being Westerners, Grace and I lost our appetite. Since Indians are extremely hospitable and sensitive to making guests comfortable and having them enjoy food, we managed to eat some with our hands, sitting on the floor as was customary in India.

Meanwhile we had become a curiosity, and people could not decide whether to watch us or the goddess.

Rumor had spread that we had come all the way from America to be with the goddess, and a man asked us how long it had taken to come from the U.S. We then explained that we were living in Delhi.

After dinner we were invited to the blue house of Satyapal's sister where she had prepared a room for us. The dusty room had two cots with thin mattresses where we put our sleeping bags. There was no closet, chest of drawers or table. Since we were extremely tired, we got a good night's sleep, but the following evening we placed our sleeping bags on the roof, which was cooler and had a lovely view.

The next morning we returned to the goddess, who according to Satyapal was in a trance. She was no longer swinging her body and was glued to the same spot with her eyes closed. I was convinced that she was exhausted and sleeping. Her disciples insisted that she was meditating. "A goddess never sleeps," said a man when I inquired.

Later that afternoon the performance of the previous day was repeated. A young girl approached us and said that the goddess would grant us a short interview. We were delighted. I went to a side door, took off my shoes and asked her, "I would like to know how and when you first found out that you were the reincarnation of a goddess."

The girl translated my question into Hindi and her answer was, "This is a long story, which I cannot tell you now."

"Perhaps you can tell me what miracles you have performed," I continued.

She did not answer. Through the interpreter she said that I should ask something about my future. I was not prepared for this nor was I curious to know my future from her.

After pleasantly posing for photos for Grace, which amused me, she closed the interview. "I am very busy now, as it is time for the pilgrimage. Come back later and I shall show you my land, take you to my fields."

We did not take her up on this offer but learned that she was very rich. Apparently this Indian goddess had many material possessions which she had acquired by receiving gifts and money from her followers. I was disillusioned.

Later we visited an ashram, where Swami Satya Devi, a follower of Gandhi, met us. A very intelligent man, he had lived in the U.S. and had written his autobiography in Hindi. He asked Grace if the book could be published in English in the U.S.; he believed that a healthy body was a prerequisite to a healthy mind and that America should be accepting some spiritualism.

Before continuing our journey to Rishikes, a quiet place surrounded by forested hills, Satyapal insisted that we bathe in the Ganges. Indians believe that if you bathe in the Ganges, you wash off your sins. We saw many "sadus" (holy men) walking along the road covered in ashes asking alms from the people. We trekked many miles before we found a sandy beach without people where it seemed safe to take a swim. After bathing, we also took a little bottle of water from the river as, according to Indians, Ganges water has properties that will cure any disease. It seemed to me, however, that the dirt could kill rather than cure you.

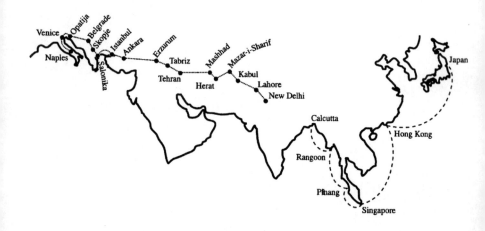

Sangola—Freighter Juliane took from Japan to Calcutta

With Robin Bannerjee, the ship's doctor

With Peggy in Rangoon

Satya and Urmila at their wedding in
Muzafarnagar

Juliane with Urmila, the bride at the
wedding

Sadus in Rishikesh

FROM INDIA TO
EUROPE BY CAR
1952

AFGHANISTAN

Little was known about Afghanistan in 1952. Hans and Paul, two Swiss journalists, decided to return to Switzerland via Afghanistan. When I had met them in Delhi, where I had finished my work at the United States Information Service, I persuaded them to take me along in their car. A photographer who had made the trip to India with them was going to Sri Lanka, so I knew there was space for a third person.

Our transportation was "Lulubelle," a 1950 Chevrolet which had brought the two s young men to India several months before. Both were in their mid-twenties. They lived in Zurich. Paul, in addition to being a free lance journalist, was a very good auto mechanic. In my opinion, they were typical Swiss—honest, reliable, with a dry sense of humor.

I looked forward to the adventure, even though they had warned me that it would be a rough trip into the unknown. When they talked about the difficulties, such as thirst and hunger, poor roads, sleeping in the car or tents with no washing facilities, it didn't mean much to me. Indeed it went in and out of my ears.

The car was loaded with four jerry cans for gas, water bags, cooking utensils, a pup tent, sleeping bags, spare parts for the car as well as two extra tires. The food we carried consisted mainly of a three-week supply of spaghetti and some cans of sardines.

Our first stop after leaving Delhi was Amritsar, which we reached after driving through a sandstorm for a few hours. The strong wind had felled many trees, so the car had to slalom through the road. Amritsar is the holy city of the Sikhs with its huge golden temple.

Shortly after leaving the town, we came to the border of India and Pakistan. There was no problem leaving India, but the Pakistan border agents insisted on examining each piece of luggage thoroughly. It seemed that some Swiss travelers had come through this border some weeks before and when they got to the Indian border, the Indians found that they had smuggled gold. Now the Pakistanis were sure that all Swiss were smugglers.

We continued to Lahore, the capital of West Punjab, a lovely city with broad avenues and many beautiful mosques and gardens. But there we had another surprise. The road to Peshawar was closed to foreigners because of rumors of war; only army vehicles and ambulances were allowed to travel. We could go by train but not by car, we were told. That of course was not our plan. Therefore we waited until nightfall and zoomed through the many checkpoints. Guards yelled in Urdu, which we did not understand. We got to Peshawar without being shot at.

In Peshawar we encountered the tall, often fierce looking Pathans dressed in mid-thigh shirts, voluminous trousers and multimeter lengths of cloth wound around the head as a turban. Most of the Pathans carried modern guns. The women were usually veiled and wore pantaloons. Their legs and arms were always covered. Some wore burkas like we later saw in Afghanistan.

The Afghan border is not far from Peshawar. From there the road to Kabul leads over the legendary Khyber Pass. I was thrilled to travel over the Khyber Pass, having learned about the violent history of this land route. Conquering armies had used the Pass as an entry point to their invasions. It was also a major trade route for centuries. As far back as 326 BC, Alexander the Great and his army marched through the Khyber to reach the plains of India. Later, Persian, Mongol and Tartar armies forced their way through the Khyber bringing Islam to India. Centuries later, India became part of the British Empire and British troops defended the Pass from the Indian side.

Of course a special permit was required. It was granted once the official had gathered vital statistics about us and our ancestors. We were not to stop on the road over the Khyber Pass, and were not allowed to take photos. The officials told us that the road was poor—a slight understatement.

As soon as we crossed the Pakistan border a dirt road led over a barren, stony plain, through the bed of a ravine. It first ascended and then by an easy zigzag descended to the river. The road went from about 1000 feet to 6000 feet behind which we saw higher snow-covered mountains. Every few miles there was a sentry making sure nobody stopped or took pictures.

The Pathans, also called Pashtuns, were and still are tribesmen living in this quasi-independent area called Pashtunistan. Here the gun is the law. All these ferocious-looking fellows carried guns. I felt somewhat ill at ease if not exactly scared. I found little comfort in thinking about the single pistol that was hidden in the trunk of

Lulubelle. Occasionally we would meet a truck, and when the road was extremely bad and the truck got stuck, the passengers had to get out and push. More frequently however, people traveled on mules, donkeys or camels.

In a little hamlet, near the top of the Khyber Pass some tribesmen stopped us. They did not speak any European language that we knew. We had to leave the car and follow one of the men at the point of his rifle. We entered a mud hut where a man in a mixture of a uniform and the usual voluminous trousers and huge turban began to question us in their language. We didn't understand a word. We showed our papers and passports to no effect. He could not read. More half-uniformed men appeared, greeted our interrogator, disappeared, came back, talked some more. I was worried, wondering how all this would end. After two hours we were ushered back to the car. We had passed the test, whatever it was, and to my great relief were permitted to proceed.

The capital of the country

We bypassed the town of Jalalabad and proceeded to Kabul. Shortly before reaching Kabul the road improved considerably. A German company was remaking it with bulldozers and pneumatic drills.

The only hotel that existed, the "Kabul," was gloomy and not very clean. Yet there were beds in the rooms and the antiquated bathrooms had running water. The hotel's restaurant served dry rice, dried meat and the flat Persian loaves of bread. Though it was the capital of the country, Kabul had no amenities of even a small

European town that I had known, for example Agen in France.

Few Indian or Pakistani towns looked so desolate. There was a main street where old cars crawled from time to time. The rows of concrete houses were rather dilapidated. The rest of the city consisted mainly of mud houses. Except for the "downtown" district, everywhere the high walls concealed the houses and the women.

This was about 11 years before the ruler, King Mohammad Zahir Shah, whose family had ruled Afghanistan for two centuries, set out to transform the backward nation into a modern state. It was before the government encouraged women to shed the all-enveloping burka or chador.

Women, primarily in the cities, were forbidden by law to walk in the streets without the chador, which is not just a veil, as required in Arab countries. The garment was most frequently of white cotton, sometimes silken underneath. It started with a little embroidered cap which fitted snugly on the head. It covered the face and body to the ankles. Only two small slits for the eyes allowed the ladies to see. The front panel went over the face and hung down to the waist.

To me this outfit seemed a little spooky because you can't see the person. Beneath this phantom looking garment, the wealthier women of Kabul often wore European dresses, sometimes the latest Paris fashion. High heels and nylon-stockinged feet could be seen peeping from the burka. Even ten year-old girls wore it.

Should a man dare to approach a lady in the street, he would be thrown into jail. At home, the ladies discarded the burka. Only her husband, servants and other women could see them thus divested. I bought a white-blue embroidered burka in the market, but as a foreigner I did not have to wear it. However, out of respect, I wore a headscarf over my hair.

While in Kabul, our main activity was to find out how to reach the Iranian border. We visited numerous ministries and government offices and received a dozen different answers. Nobody seemed to know anything definite about the state of the roads and the availability of gas along the way. We learned that there was a road through Southern Afghanistan via Kandahar. However, we preferred to cross Northern Afghanistan. If there were roads, the trip would be shorter, cooler and more beautiful, as it would lead close to high mountains and the Soviet Union's border.

A Swiss engineer told us that he had been to Mazar-i-Sharif by jeep. What was beyond, neither he nor anybody else seemed to know. I went to the U.S. Embassy and told an official what we were planning to do.

"If you get through," he said, "be sure to let us know" as we as well as the Afghan government would like to know if any roads through the North are passable."

In spite of all the discouraging information, my two companions decided to take this untraveled route through the north. We required a permit. In Afghanistan you needed one for everything you wanted to do or didn't want to do. A permit was required to stay a few days in Kabul, to travel and for gas coupons. With the help of an Afghan student who spoke English, which the officials did not, we received enough gasoline coupons to reach Masar-i-Sharif.We also had procured a letter to an official there, who was then to give us further gas coupon permits, if any gasoline existed beyond that town.

The Buddhas of Bamiyan

Shortly after leaving Kabul, the temperature dropped. At night it was actually cold. The scenery was lovely. We were pleased with our decision and were richly rewarded driving along the Hindu Kush Range in a marvelous countryside. Broad high deserts were framed by snowy mountains. Rivers born in high peaks rushed through the valleys and mountain passes. Fields of poppies and corn flowers, like giant Persian carpets, stretched before us. At times we passed through narrow canyons, almost touching the reddish rocks that flanked the roads.

Camel and donkey caravans, monkeys and colorful pedestrians of different racial origins, blended with this romantic background. I saw Afghans having Mongol features, others with blue eyes and light hair. Once or twice a wedding party on camels passed by with bells ringing. The women were dressed in bright costumes and did not wear the burka nor hide their attractive faces behind veils. Rarely did we pass through a village or hamlet. Here Afghans were primarily nomads. They had russet tents and grazing sheep. Some used caves in the rocks as shelter. Incredible ruins of forts, some built by Alexander the Great, were scattered here and there.

We reached Bamiyan with the two huge cliff-side Buddhas. They were the first known examples of the massive Buddha images that later spread throughout Asia. One was 175 feet and the other 120 feet high. The two sandstone statues were erected at a caravan stop along the fabled Silk Route to China. These Buddhas were the best-known product of the fusion of European and Asian art that flourished in Afghanistan and Northern Pakistan between the fourth and seventh centuries. I saw an inscription over the taller figure. On each side of its niche was a staircase leading to a chamber near the head.

While Hans and Paul were busy with the car, I decided to explore the interior of this Buddha and climbed up on the stairs to the head. Then I got lost in the big head. Only after much searching did I grope my way back through his arms and legs.

According to Jet van Krieken of the Society for the Preservation of Afghanistan's Cultural Heritage, the two Buddhas had faces and hands covered in gold, a style familiar to many tourists who have visited the Buddhas of Thailand and Burma. Shortly before the Taliban destroyed them, van Krieken observed, "It seems a miracle that these incredible Buddhas have more or less survived in a country in which they have become strangers who were not able to flee." Fifty years before their destruction, I felt that way about my visit in Bamiyan.

I was terribly shocked when I learned about the destruction of these Buddhas not too long ago. How could the Taliban be so ruthless and have no respect for history and art? I could hardly believe it and was very upset. On the other hand, I felt that I had been privileged to have seen them. Other persons no longer have the opportunity to view these huge, magnificent Buddhas.

We found a hotel in Bamiyan, a large building on top of a hill, built for French archeologists and apparently also kept up by them in the past. But it was neglected at this time. The manager showed us many empty rooms. We chose two which had at least part of the windows left. We exchanged our sleeping bags for the unwashed sheets. From the broken windows, I had an excellent view of the Buddhas and the snowcapped peaks.

The following morning we tried to get some gasoline. The Swiss journalists showed the coupons to some persons in the town's center and for a few hours pleaded in sign language without success. Eventually, we gathered that they wanted us to return to the hotel, which we did. After waiting for a few more hours and just about giving up hope, three men arrived with big barrels of gasoline. They poured the gasoline into our tank only after we had surrendered our coupons and had paid them.

A small caravan had also stopped at the hotel. In the evening I joined the women, and we tried to communicate. They were very curious about my clothes and all touched my skirt and blouse wanting to know what I wore under them. They laughed a lot and I smiled in answer to their questions.

It was not often that we found a hotel during our journey. Usually, at night, we would park the car in a meadow, and after moving out the luggage, creep into the car to sleep. Sometimes, we would just sleep in our sleeping bags in the fields. In the morning a crowd of nomads and peasants would collect around the car, stare at us and chatter loudly. It took some time to get friendly with these sightseers. Our actions would be watched in wonder and speculation, especially when we brushed our teeth or brewed the morning tea on the little camp-stove.

As we continued, the roads got worse. One day we drove about 250 km, the next 230 km, in a ten-to twelve-hour day. We saw few people while driving along. Afghanistan had only a little over eight million inhabitants in 1952. (Now there are approximately 26 million.)

It was very warm and dry and I was constantly thirsty. I daydreamed of milk and juices as we drove through the country. Often when we stopped, we were too tired to set up camp and eat our spaghetti. Frequently I went to sleep thirsty and hungry. I usually sat in back of the Chevrolet, while Hans and Paul shared the driving. For entertainment we discussed the merits of a Chevrolet, my companions pointing out that it was assembled in Switzerland, while I insisted it was after all an American car.

One day perhaps 500 km from Kabul we met a European cyclist. The young Frenchman had left France by bike two years earlier. When asked about roads and gasoline, he thought there were no passable roads and gasoline after Masar-i-Sharif. At his suggestion, we then visited the camp of French archeologists where he was working temporarily.

They were as amazed to see us as we were happy to see them. A celebration was called for. The lukewarm beer tasted like cold champagne. The expedition was excavating some Greek temples which they showed us proudly. The French had a monopoly of archeology in the country, but lack of funds had recently made them invite Americans to join.

"No problem to Mazar-i-Sharif," said the director, "but after that, Inschallah (God Willing)."

In spite of such discouraging information we continued our adventure.

Caravans and camels

When we reached Mazar-i-Sharif the next day we stopped in the center of town in order to find an official to whom we could present our letter requesting additional gasoline coupons. By luck, we had stopped right in front of the police station. Two policemen came out, looked at our letter and then accompanied us to the special official who was in charge of such documents.

The official studied the letter and then gave us the necessary coupons. To our relief, he assured us that gasoline would be available in Meymaned on the way to Herat as well as in Herat, the third largest city in Afghanistan. If this was true, and we did not lose our way too often, we felt we could reach our goal.

The one hotel in the town had rooms available. It was a little better than the hotel in Bamiyan, and I was glad to sleep in a bed for a change. The other guests were five Russian men. The Russians did not talk to us, but the hotel manager told us that they were surveying the town and the roads, as they were planning to construct a road from the Uzbekistan Soviet Republic.

Refreshed and loaded with gasoline, water and bread we proceeded with renewed optimism. Soon, after about 60 km, the dirt road changed to a path and then at the next crossroad, four paths met. We waited till a few people came by on donkeys or mules. Asking for directions to Andhui, the next little town we wanted to reach, did not help. No matter what direction we pointed, they would nod affirmatively. So we had to experiment on our own.

The first path ended abruptly. The second path started somewhat better, but after a few miles turned to sand. All day we drove in circles, mostly in first gear. Would we have enough gasoline to get to Herat if we continued in this manner? A swarm of locusts descended, which added to our misery. They were so dense that we could barely see through the windshield.

As we did not encounter any other person, we returned to the village which we had passed prior to the intersection of the four paths. Once there, we could not communicate. Finally, in desperation, I wrote "Andhui" in the Cyrillic alphabet in the sand of a street. That seemed to work. I was amazed that my one year of college Russian could be so useful. A peasant accompanied us to show us the way to Andhui. It was

FROM RUCKSACK TO BACKPACK 69

one of the four paths we had previously tried and given up as impossible.

The path was getting soggier and soggier. The mud got so deep the car got stuck. We pushed and pulled without success. Luckily an Afghan on a donkey appeared and helped to dig us out. A few miles later we got stuck again. This time the camel drivers of a caravan helped. They pointed to their camels, wet and muddy to the knees, to indicate what was ahead. It was dark by then, so we tried to sleep in the car waiting for daybreak. The next day we continued to creep through the mud, covering a distance of 15 km in two hours.

Next there was a wide river, more like a lake, to cross. A truck loaded with people had just come through. So this was the right road. But Chevrolets are not amphibious. While I watched the car, Hans and Paul waded into the water to find a shallow spot. The crowd in the truck shouted with excitement, urging us on. The two Swiss decided to try and ford the river. Cameras and other belongings were unloaded for me to guard while they drove the car. The car stopped. All passengers of the truck stepped into the water and pushed and pulled. Hours of combined efforts didn't get us anywhere and the truck left us.

What to do? Reluctantly I suggested that we should exchange the car in the water for some camels and continue our journey. Hans agreed that we might have to do that. But for the moment, we would just have to wait for the camels.

Finally, after a couple of hours, a man on a camel arrived. He looked at the car in the water, made some noises and disappeared. Not long after that several men on camels appeared with our savior. They lashed two camels in front of the car and in no time they succeeded in shifting her.

We were extremely grateful to these people, yet they refused to accept any money for their effort. This had also been true of the passengers and driver of the truck that had tried to help. Throughout our hazardous journey, the people were always willing to help but would never accept any rewards, except perhaps a few Russian cigarettes that we had purchased. Thenceforth we followed the tracks of the truck, skirting a wet ditch which once had been the principal road. We reached the little town of Andhui in an eleven-hour day covering about 70 km.

The town, which was about 15 km from the Soviet border, was once an important trading post. It was almost deserted and many of its buildings were in ruins. The trade with Russia apparently had stopped in the last years. Since we were exhausted we decided to rest and stayed there two nights in the town's only hotel.

The next day we set out for the bazaar. As we approached the center of town, the entire police force of Andhui, consisting of eight men, gathered to protect us from the curiosity of the inhabitants. A large crowd had gathered to see the three foreigners. Only with the policeman's pushing the crowd apart could we proceed in the narrow streets. The people were a mixture of Usbeks, Tajiks, Hazara, Pashtuns and others. They seemed curious about us but friendly. Few women were in the streets. The fact that I was a woman didn't seem to bother the crowd. With our bodyguard we wandered through the bazaar. We each bought a carpet, produced either here or in one of the neighboring countries. The commander of the police even bargained for a good deal. As we learned later, he had definitely helped us to get a good price. It was not like in most tourist areas where the guide or helper gets a commission, which makes the item more expensive.

We crossed one stream after another when we continued our journey. In two days we had to ford 14 streams, rivers, small lakes or mud holes of various width and depth. As before, we would wade through the water to find a shallow and hard spot before diving through. More often than not, the car stopped. We would wait till somebody came along. Such helper, after looking at the situation, usually vanished and returned an hour or so later with reinforcement. We had learned to adopt the local practice of waiting and not worrying. While the Chevrolet sat in the middle of a stream, we would bathe our feet, wash the car or read a book. This routine was almost refreshing.

Leading up to Herat the diverse landscape included plains ringed by rugged mountains, small villages of mud-walled dwellings as well as mountain passes of the Bandi-Turkestan mountains which reached up to 16,000 feet. Not until entering Herat, were we certain that we did not have to return to Kabul. The road might have stopped at any time, a river proven impossible to cross, gasoline not available or a spring of the car might have broken.

Herat had many ruins of Greek strongholds, which were the glory and wonder of the East. A beautiful hotel, a modern white building with a splendid garden, welcomed us. Every room had three layers of Persian or Afghan rugs. Bathrooms had showers. Electric switches could be seen at every wall. The living room even had a Swedish refrigerator. However, the refrigerator was out of order; the doors and windows did not close; the water was not running, The entire building had no electricity. Nevertheless, these luxuries were pleasant to look at. For the first time since we had left Kabul, our diet of rice and meat—or the canned spaghetti which we had brought—was eked out with some lilliputian apples and cucumbers.

I went to the post office in order to send a telegram to my parents in Los Angeles. Surely they were very worried that they had no news from me since Kabul. I wrote the telegram but the postal clerk did not know that there was a town by the name of Los Angeles in the United States. After much discussion with his superior, he told me that the only place in America that a telegram could be sent to from Herat was New York. So I sent a telegram to a relative in New York, asking her to phone my parents.

We had crossed Northern Afghanistan, which had not turned out to be the shortest route. It had taken us 12 days to cover the thousand kilometers from Kabul. Hopefully, the roads would be better in Iran.

Indeed, Afghanistan had been an adventure. I was glad that I had made it and could not forget this wonderful country with its snow-covered peaks, its broad high deserts and its green valleys.

But above all what had impressed me most were the polite and hospitable people, always willing to help. Even the officials and bureaucrats were very cordial, and the soldiers guarding public buildings with their guns had often a dark red rose at the mouth of their weapons.

Lulubelle, the 1950 Chevrolet that took us
from India to Europe on a Pass between
Kabul and Bamiyan

Tribesmen at Khyber Pass

Hans and Paul having lunch

Street in Kabul

Afghan Men and Boys

Buddha in Bamyan

Huts of the people in the country

Fully loaded bus before fording a river

The passengers of the bus helped to pull
Lulubelle from the river

Afghan girls in Herat

IRAN

Soon the road which was an important trade route between Afghanistan and Iran improved. However, we had a minor mishap. At a speed of 25 miles per hour, the baggage hold from the roof of the car came loose. The tent, spare tires, sleeping bags and the newly acquired Afghan carpets slipped over the hood to the ground. Miraculously we didn't drive over our belongings. We loaded everything on the car, which took us more than an hour.

The Afghan border consisted of a few houses and a Farsi sign. The place seemed deserted. We blew our horn. Nothing happened. Finally an officer appeared. He looked at our passports and papers, glanced at the car and let us proceed.

We drove through no-man's land for almost an hour till we arrived in a little town which lay on the Iranian border. People gathered around us with much excitement. It seemed a novelty to see an American car in 1952. Only a minor official was present at the customs house, and he explained mainly through sign language that we had to be inspected by his superior. This man, however, was not available. Since it was afternoon, neither the time for dinner nor the customary siesta, we were wondering where to find him. Along with our escort, we walked from house to house looking for the superior. After visiting his home and the house that was probably that of his mistress, we stopped at several cafes. In one we found him with a young woman.

The official, a middle-aged man with dark, curly hair

and sharp brown eyes, searched our car thoroughly. Since Iran was a police state, our cameras were sealed, and we were forbidden to take photos. While the search took place, the women living in the customs house were peeking from many windows. Should Hans and Paul glance at them, they would quickly cover their faces.

When the search was completed, the official served us tea and begged us to stay overnight in his town. "It is too late to drive on," he said. My companions thanked him for the hospitality but preferred to drive on and camp in the countryside. Before we continued our journey, the local newspaper reporter interviewed us in French. French was the most common European language spoken by officials and intellectuals at that time.

Every few hours there were checkpoints along the roads. We had to show our passports and papers whenever they stopped us. Dr. Mohammad Mossadeq was prime minister at the time, nationalizing Iran's oil industry, and Iran was under martial law. A year later the CIA organized a coup to get Mossadeq out and returned the Shah to the throne. The oil industry was denationalized but the former British monopoly was broken and the United States gained a 40 percent share in it.

The roads, though rough and neglected, were better in Iran. We covered the 1,000 km from Mashhad to Teheran in a little over three days, while it had taken us twelve days to cover almost the same distance in Afghanistan. The countryside was sandy and barren. The heat was intense. Water was scarce, and our food consisted mainly of bread and cucumbers, which we bought in the market. One or two flat tires a day was not uncommon. While camping in the desert, the car often got stuck in the sand. We always gathered stones to place under the wheels, then pushed and pulled till the Chevrolet was on the road again.

A stream of animals consisting of camels, donkeys, mules, horses, sheep and bullocks flowed by along the road. From time to time automobiles approached, producing a dense cloud of dust. The most pleasant surprise was the neat, modern gas stations of the former Anglo-Iranian Oil Company. They resembled U.S. gas stations except for the absence of restrooms and Coca-Cola. Gas in Iran was about 33 U.S. cents a gallon.

We stopped briefly in Mashhad, Iran's holiest city, sacred to the Shiites. The Shrine of Emam Reza and the surrounding buildings known collectively as Astan-e Quods-e Razavi were absolutely beautiful. The golden dome and the two golden minarets impressed me very much. Indeed long after we had left Mashhad we remembered this golden structure under the deep blue, shimmering sky.

Non-Muslims were not allowed to enter the mosque but could visit many of the other buildings and gardens. Even though I was dressed in long trousers and a long-sleeved shirt and was in the company of two men, I was very uncomfortable. Men around me seemed very unfriendly. I could not understand what they said but the remarks and expressions on their faces were extremely hostile.

This was my first lesson of the hostility of Persians

toward "improperly" dressed foreign women, without the "chardar." A few weeks later in Tabriz, the second largest city of Iran, I had a more threatening encounter.

My two companions were at a garage supervising the repair of the Chevrolet. Oriental bazaars intrigued me, so I took the opportunity to explore unaccompanied the enormous market. Soon I got hopelessly lost in the turning and twisting alleys. Hundreds of men gathered around me and followed me. I didn't know where the exit was, and I didn't dare to ask. They started to shout. Some spat at me and a few threw stones. I was very scared, but what could I do? I just continued to walk with my eyes looking straight ahead and prayed that the stones would not hit me and that I would escape unharmed. Some stones almost touched my feet. Finally, after more than an hour, which seemed an eternity, I saw an opening to the street. I escaped. The men did not follow me. Never had I been so glad to get out unscathed, and I joined my Swiss friends in the garage.

Tabriz, which had been occupied by the Russians several times in the first half of the 20th century, was anti-foreign and anti-American. I believe that the hostility was not directed toward me as an American, since they did not know my nationality, but as an "impure woman" since my European dress without the veil was not appropriate in the eyes of the Iranians.

Teheran

In Teheran, Hans and Paul stayed with some Swiss friends while I found a pension which was recommended

by the American Embassy. We had to rest, clean up and
the car needed repair, so we remained twelve days.

It was a nice change to be by myself for most of this
time. The three of us had gotten along well, but I looked
forward to wandering around Teheran by myself, visiting
places on my own and perhaps learning more about Iran.

Teheran at the time was a metropolis of about a million
people located in the valley of the Alborz Mountains.
These dry mountains, mostly devoid of vegetation, at
points as high as the American Rockies, were all ridges,
valleys, rocks and sand. Sometimes they seemed a flat,
impenetrable, dun-colored wall, separating Teheran from
the world. At other times they changed color. More often
of a gray or maroon color, at times they appeared purple
and pink, with blue or green patches.

The city did not have much charm. It had broad
avenues, intersecting at right angles. Imposing
government buildings, combining native and Western
architecture, gave Teheran a modern character. It offered
many a curious contrast. Its traffic included a mixture
of streamlined American automobiles, fleets of small
British-built taxis, pushcarts, wagons, buses, war-surplus
trucks and burros. Even in the city's main square a flock
of sheep and goats, or perhaps camels in from the desert,
momentarily stopped the traffic.

Though boasting broad streets, traffic lights, dial
telephones and pretentious buildings, Teheran still
lacked sanitary water and sewage systems. Water from
the mountains flowed in its stone gutters, called "jules."
Children waded in it and animals drank from it. No
foreigner touched "jule" water, nor did those who could

afford a well. The more affluent also patronized the swarm of water peddlers who filled their two-wheeled tank carts at city wells. The pension where I stayed had "embassy" water—water from the private well of the American Embassy. The mass of people, however, used "jule" water.

Western dress was predominant, unlike in other cities and towns of Iran. Men wore tailored business suits, women, dresses. A minority of older women clung to the flowing "chadar." In any crowd, only the mullah, in a turban and black gown, served to remind the visitor where he was.

Teheran was a city of rags and riches. Palaces and pretentious walled villas dotted the city and its northern suburbs. On sidewalks, well-dressed men brushed elbows with barefoot porters, well diggers and other laborers. Flanking the main road, south to the shrine of Rey, families lived in caves. However, I found few beggars in the streets. I learned that they were fed and housed in rehabilitation centers.

In addition to visiting the covered bazaar, I went to various museums, the library and the Government Arts and Crafts Institution. Here they tried to preserve the ancient arts, especially the designs of Persia. I saw how carpets, brocades, tiles and inlaid bronzes were made. There was also a wood-carving and an ivory section. Some of the best Persian artists were gathered in this Institute built by Reza Shah Pahlevi to teach their skills to the next generation and thus preserve Persian art.

One night I witnessed a performance of "Zurkhaneh." It was a mixture of gymnastics, music and religion. At

times it was very rhythmic, at times it seemed more like
a prayer. Fifteen men standing around the perimeter of
a lowered pit performed a series of highly ritualized
dances and feats of strength. The leader beat the drum
or recited poetry. The exhibition included juggling and
many different movements. Coordination, perfect
control of muscles, strength and rhythm were all
gloriously displayed in this performance, which dated
back hundreds of years. There were few Iranian women
present, but in the company of a male friend, the
performers and audience didn't seem to mind my
presence.

Along with my Swiss companions I spent a lot of time
in the offices of the police and other officials. We were
soon entangled in the red tape and bureaucracy of Iran.
As in Afghanistan we needed numerous permits and had
to fill out dozens of forms, which had to be accompanied
with our pictures. Many forms had to be translated into
Farsi and that meant an extra charge. A permit to travel
through military regions on the way to Turkey, as well
an exit visa, was required. I planned to go by bus to
Isfahan for which another document had to be produced.
Since at the time Iranians were rather anti-American,
they were in no hurry to give the necessary papers. They
loved to make you come back several times before they
turned over the precious documents. One day the official
was out for lunch, the next he could not find the permit,
the third was a holiday and the fourth, another person
had to sign it. If we had been willing to squeeze a nice
sum of money into the hand of the appropriate official,
the permit would have been given in a day or two. I was

told that one American, who had "tipped" the police, always got to town in no time from his home. The police knew his car and all traffic lights changed to green when he approached.

Isfahan

Finally I received my "laissez-passer" (permit) to travel to Isfahan. I had learned that this city was perhaps one of the finest in the Islamic world, therefore I decided to visit it for a few days instead of spending more time in Teheran waiting for the car's repair. So alone, I took a bouncing bus for about ten hours to Isfahan.

It was a dusty and rugged trip. My fellow passengers were peasants, merchants and other common people who were extremely friendly. Even though our conversation was somewhat limited, though a few knew some French, they wanted to know all about America after learning that I was from the United States. The men and women tried to make me as comfortable as possible. The bus driver insisted that I share his lunch, which consisted of flat bread filled with minced meat and vegetables. Others also offered nuts and fruit.

We crossed miles of desolate country often with strange geologic formations. There were few dwellings. Camels and donkeys and a few shepherds with their sheep traveled on the roads. A high plateau followed the desert, which gave way to hills close to Isfahan.

Shah Abbas the Great, a contemporary of Queen Elizabeth I, made Isfahan his capital and adorned it with architectural jewels. I was overwhelmed by the beauty of this city, not regretting for one minute the long trip in the rattling bus.

Along the Maidan-i-Shah square (now Emam Khomeini square) I saw three of the most superb buildings perhaps ever erected by men. The three symmetric mosques with their elaborate brickwork and turquoise domes stood out against the clear blue sky of the city. The buildings were adorned with tile-covered minarets on their sides. The tiles of the mosques and minarets were mosaics, turquoise and lapis lazuli in color, delicate in design and with exquisite lettering. The square hummed with activity. Merchants, running a curb market, displayed miscellaneous wares from pins to old door hinges. Whenever trade slackened they lolled on bright rugs, sipped tea and smoked water pipes.

In gaping wonder I walked around the square to see these masterpieces of old Persian architecture from every angle. On the other side of the square was the Al Qapu Palace, a small palace that the Shah used. It was much damaged and badly in need of repair. I climbed its roof and had an unforgettable view of the splendor of Isfahan and its surroundings.

Of course I also visited the bazaar. Holes in the street's vaulted roofs admitted bright shafts of sunlight that resembled batteries of spotlights. In the section of the metalworkers, thousands of hammers tapped a ceaseless anvil chorus. In hundreds of small workshops, boys tended bellows and roughed out work, while craftsmen fashioned delicate pitchers, ornamental trays and samovars. The carpet-makers wove with quick, practiced hands accompanied with much chatter.

Unfortunately, I did not have time to visit Shiraz and Persepolis. I returned to Teheran and continued our trip to Turkey with my Swiss companions.

TURKEY

Once we passed the Turkish border, we were greeted by a different country than we had expected. Though most of Turkey is in Asia, the atmosphere seemed more European.

As we traveled, our conversation went beyond what we saw and our plans. Paul talked about his teaching at a high school in Zurich. I told my companions that I had learned to ski in St. Moritz, Switzerland, when I was eleven years old.

Not far from the border was Mount Ararat, almost 17,000 feet high, the traditional resting place of Noah's Arc, according to legend. Unfortunately the soaring volcano was shrouded in dark clouds. Nevertheless, I was thrilled to be so close to the famous mountain.

Instead of desert we now passed through a range of bare, jagged mountains and a table-flat expanse of wheat fields. A little further down the road there were green valleys, fertile brown soil and lovely prairie flowers. Small towns had concrete buildings with architecture that resembled that of France or Switzerland.

The climate was pleasant. Instead of the scorching heat, it was cool, and heavy rainstorms were not infrequent.

The well-kept gravel roads were being improved by bulldozers. American machinery was used on the highways. Turkey benefited directly from the Marshal Plan. Yet we met few private cars; traffic consisted mainly of army vehicles, jeeps, pick-ups and tractors.

Eastern Turkey resembled one big military camp.

Miles of barracks and training fields were visible all along the road to Ankara. Often we watched the Turkish army being trained in the nearby camps. Turkey had just joined NATO that year.

We passed through Erzurum, an important trading town and headquarters of one of the three Turkish armies. The town was located on a high plateau and was the largest in Eastern Turkey. It had some fine Seljuk Turkish buildings, including several mosques. The streets in the old town were alive. Tattered shepherds with beards and leathery faces were hustling herds of oxen and goats through the main thoroughfare.

Ataturk's reforms regarding the emancipation of women had not yet succeeded in this part of the country. Older women still wore the veil, while younger ones were dressed in red pantaloons with head shawls close to their faces. In the coffeehouses where the men sat for hours drinking coffee, playing cards and discussing local affairs, women were not present. No women were seen in restaurants.

It was in the town of Erzincan, west of Erzurum, that I was directly confronted with the eastern Turkish prejudice against women. It had been raining, and we were unable to cross a stream on our way westward. We met an American officer, who was there because of NATO, when we returned to the center of town.

"Why don't you stay overnight in Erzincan?" said the captain, a pale and handsome man in his 30s, with light eyes and hair. "The next day some of us have to go to Siwas in a pick-up. If you get stuck, we could easily get you out."

"Thank you," answered Hans. "That sounds just fine."

We found a small hotel and stayed overnight. The captain, an interpreter and two other American officers then joined us for dinner, vodka and raki, the national alcoholic drink made from the residue of grapes left over from wine making.

When we entered the restaurant, every guest stared at me in great surprise. I felt very uncomfortable, yet safe in the company of six men. To the Turks in the restaurant, my actions seemed outrageous. The waiter took the order of my companions but refused to serve me.

"This lady is only passing through our town," said the interpreter, a small, dark man with a bushy mustache. "She has no home where she could cook a meal." Reluctantly, the waiter took my order through the interpreter and served me with a sour face.

We continued the next day to Sivas without any trouble. We stopped at a gas station for fuel and to change a flat tire. A gray-haired man with intense dark eyes and dark brows, the father of the attendant, wanted to talk to me. He could speak some German.

"Where are you from?" he asked with a brilliant smile.

"I am from America."

"What brings you to our country?"

"We are coming from Iran and wanted to visit Turkey on our way to Western Europe," I said. "We like Turkey very much."

"You are the first foreigner I have ever met," he said. "Now that I have met an American lady, I understand why Americans and Turks have become such good friends in such a short time."

He refused to take money for the work of his son, and we paid only for the gas. Everywhere we found the people most friendly, warm and helpful to travelers.

The heartland of Anatolia, close to Ankara, seemed deserted. Rolling plains were surrounded by baked yellow hills. We must have passed close to Capadoccia, but did not realize it at the time. Capadoccia is famed for its weird geology. Deep layers of volcanic ash settled into easily carved tufa, which has offered shelter to people creating cave-homes from prehistoric times. During the early Christian era it became a popular retreat for hermits and later for other Christians fleeing persecution by Romans, and later by Muslims. Only forty years later, when I visited Turkey again and admired the area of Capadoccia, did I realize that we had been close to this famous tourist attraction.

Ankara was a government town, a modern city with wide boulevards and impressive buildings. The cafes along the streets and boulevards were filled with well-dressed people drinking coffee. The veil was not visible. There was a large park with a yachting basin, swimming pool, open-air restaurants and many shady benches named after the banks that had provided them. The city had a European atmosphere.

The drive from Ankara to Istanbul was easy and quick. We had completed our journey through Asia; only a ferry separated Asia from Europe. No bridges existed at this time over the Bosphorus, and as a thousand years before, people traveled by boat to go from Asian to

European parts of the city. These little motor boats that plied back and forth symbolized an important aspect of the city. As we drove the Chevrolet onto the ferry, admiring in wonder the blue waters of the Bosphorus, we had our first view of the European continent. The dome of the Blue Mosque and the pencil-thin minarets identified the skyline of Istanbul. I was tremendously impressed, and happy that we had succeeded in getting to this beautiful city. It was the first time I was back in Europe since I left eleven years before. I was looking forward to experiencing a Europe in peacetime.

We decided to remain in Istanbul for several days. The town was crowded, and we had difficulties finding a hotel. Eventually we located a reasonable one with vacant rooms in the center. We enjoyed sightseeing for a few days, visiting the marvelous St. Sophia, built in 532 A.D. as a mosque, the Topkapi Palace and other palaces, mosques and museums. The crowded bazaar, which lined ninety-two streets and was divided into different districts with crossroads as well as open squares and blind alleys, seemed more organized than the ones we had visited in other towns during our journey.

THE YUGOSLAV VISA

Shortly after arriving in Istanbul I went to the Yugoslav consulate to apply for a visa for Yugoslavia. My Swiss companions, who had obtained their visas in Zurich, had indicated that we had to drive through Yugoslavia before reaching Italy and Switzerland. I had tried to get the visa in both India and Teheran, but was unsuccessful. Yugoslavia had broken with the U.S.S.R. only a few years before and perhaps that was one reason the country did not want American visitors. It was still a communist country led by the dictator Tito, who had introduced "Socialist Self-Management."

Istanbul was my last chance to get the visa. The consulate was on an upper floor of an old building. As I entered, the receptionist gave me an application to fill out, then took the completed form and my photo to another room. I waited for about half an hour before being ushered into a spacious, elegantly furnished room with large windows overlooking the city.

"Why do you want to go to Yugoslavia?" asked the second secretary. He was a handsome man in his early 30s with deep-set eyes. He was meticulously dressed in a dark suit with polished shoes. He spoke impeccable French. I was surprised, as he did not fit my image of a communist.

"I have always wanted to visit your beautiful country," I answered. "I am on my way to Italy by car."

"Yes, my country is very beautiful, and I wish I could show it to you," he responded, his eyes fixed on me.

Many other questions followed such as :"Whom are

you traveling with?" "Where are you staying?" "Where are your companions?" I did not think these questions were relevant to the visa application, which had all the necessary personal information, but tried to answer them.

When he learned that I had just arrived in Istanbul, he asked me to step on the terrace, which had a splendid view of the city.

"I would like to show you Istanbul, since I cannot accompany you to my homeland."

"That would be very nice," I answered politely, while my thoughts were only on the visa. It didn't occur to me that he really meant it.

"All right, I will meet you at seven p.m. at the corner of Ikal and Burki street," said Vladimir, which he told me was his first name.

I left the consulate, wondering if I really had agreed to meet Vladimir, the communist. And if so, should I go or shouldn't I? Would I get the visa if I would let him show me the city? Obviously he did not want to be seen with an American capitalist. Otherwise he would have arranged to pick me up at my hotel. Finally my curiosity, sense of adventure and the desire to continue the journey through Yugoslavia influenced my decision to go to the place he had mentioned.

It was dark when I arrived, nervous and apprehensive, at the meeting place. What am I doing here on this dark street in a strange city? Shouldn't I return to the safety of my hotel?

I was just about to return to the hotel, when five minutes after seven o'clock, a large black car with diplomatic license plates stopped in front of me like in a Hitchcock movie. "Jump in," said the diplomat.

The next few hours we drove all over the city and the shores of the Bosphorus. Vladimir pointed out important buildings and their history. In the darkness, the lights of the mosques, the palaces and the charming seaside villas illuminated the sky. Small villages bordered the water and boats with bright lights cruised the Bosphorus. I found the setting very romantic.

Vladimir also told me a lot about his country, stressing the beautiful places to visit, some of the attractions on our way and the country's history. He did not discuss politics, and I thought it would be wise not to ask questions as it might have had a negative influence on my getting the visa. He mentioned, however, that he had been a partisan during the war. I couldn't have had a more charming, well-educated and interesting guide.

We stopped at a restaurant many miles from the city. To reach the dining room, we had to climb more than three-dozen steep stone steps. The room had a magnificent view of the sea, but there were no other guests.

The elaborate meal consisted of "metzes," which were appetizers of several types of eggplants, delicious kebabs and dessert, a rich baklava. A tasty Turkish wine accompanied the dinner. By now I had relaxed and felt at ease in Vladimir's company.

Once back in the car he took my arm and tried to kiss me. I maneuvered to get out of the embrace, pushing him away. He finally gave up, as he realized I was seriously resisting his advances. All this time, I was wondering about my visa and passport at the consulate.

During the drive back to the city, the diplomat was as charming and pleasant as before. Shortly before reaching the street where my hotel was located he said, "It is very difficult to park right in front of your hotel, would you mind if I let you out just two blocks before?"

"Of course, that would be just fine," I answered, again confirming that he was afraid to be seen with me.

"I'll see you tomorrow morning at the consulate at eleven," were his last words when I left the car in great relief.

The next morning I went to the consulate with enormous apprehension. Vladimir received me warmly, without referring to the previous evening. It seemed as if the outing had never taken place. He handed me my passport with the visa and wished me a pleasant journey.

THE FORMER YUGOSLAVIA

Lulubelle had received new springs and I had my visa, so with my companions I continued the journey to Yugoslavia and Italy, first passing through northern Greece.

The border between Turkey and Greece was near Erdine, which the Greek call Adrianople. Then, all of a sudden, instead of getting to the Greek border, we found ourselves in front of a sign that read "Bulgaria." We quickly returned, having realized that we had taken a wrong road.

We crossed the Greek border and for more than 200 km. drove on what was considered Europe's worst road. It reminded us of the roads of Afghanistan. Holes and rocks made driving at a speed of 40 kmph like flying. Inches-thick dust seeped through the floorboards of the Chevrolet and settled on the windows like snow.

The scenery in northern Greece was spectacular. Gray mountains gaunt against the sky slanted steeply to the blue sea. Vineyards and olive groves could be seen on the terraced lower slopes. Small towns squeezed behind rock walls and the sea or perched on stony highland shoulders. Green islands in profusion were located in the sea.

Among the towns that we passed was Karalla, almost a peninsula, stretching into the water. On top of a hill was an old fortress, dominating the town below. That night we slept on the beach, not far from Salonika. In the morning we took a refreshing swim in the Aegean.

In Salonika we replenished our supplies and received

gas from the U.S. consulate at considerable savings. The city was crowded with sailors from a U.S. cruiser that was in the harbor that day.

From there to the Yugoslav border the destruction of the 1944-49 Greek civil war was visible everywhere. This area had seen some terrible guerilla fighting. Houses and bridges were in ruins. We had great difficulty finding the right trail to the Yugoslav border, as signs did not exist.

The moment we arrived at the border, we were very much aware that the country was a police state. The border had double barriers. After showing our papers the guard let us pass, but then large boulders placed zigzag on the road forced us to drive very slowly. Before the third barrier was opened, an official descended from a house on a hill, took the passports and returned more than half an hour later. Before returning the passports he checked the car and all our belongings very thoroughly. He then gave us a number of different documents and told us to stop at the Putnik in Skopje.

Skopje (now Macedonia) was the first town we passed. Putnik was the official government travel agency that was charged to assign visitors with hotel rooms, gasoline coupons and transportation. The pleasant agent, a blond muscular man in his 30s, gave us all the necessary information about the roads and gasoline. We told him that we did not need hotel accommodations, as we planned to camp, to which he had no objections.

The region was impoverished and rather gloomy, yet people seemed happy. In one village we came across a group of dancers in colorful Macedonian costumes. They were singing and dancing to the music of the local orchestra. They invited us to take part in the fun, and were glad to have their pictures taken. They spoke some French or Italian. Everywhere we found the people friendly and extremely curious about us, our car and our lives. Even though the Chevrolet had Swiss license plates, when they spotted the car they waved and shouted, "Amerikanski!"

Whenever we stopped to get gas, check the car or buy food, primarily bread and vegetables such as tomatoes and cucumbers, the locals would gather around us. Since many people in Yugoslavia outside of Macedonia spoke some German, which they probably had learned during the war, they could communicate with us.

How much does a watch cost in Switzerland? How much do you pay for a glass of beer, a loaf of bread, a pair of shoes in the United States? How much do you earn? How long do you have to work to buy a car? were some of the questions.

One person asked: "Who is better, Taft or Eisenhower?" It was during the Republican convention of 1952.

Food was cheap for us because of the favorable exchange rate. Consumer goods were scarce and expensive. The stores had little to sell and what was for sale was of very poor quality. Shoes, clothing and household goods were inferior and at least double the price of similar items in the United States or Switzerland.

A farmer told us that he had to work sixteen days to buy a working shirt.

In Belgrade we saw no well-dressed women in the streets except for a few tourists. Women wore wrinkled and baggy dresses; men wore old shirts and ill-fitting crumpled slacks. On the other hand we had a delicious meal, a five-course dinner with wine for about one dollar a person.

Many men and women frequented the numerous outdoor cafes drinking cheap beer or coffee. Yet one was conscious of the boundless energy of the nation pulling itself up by its bootstraps. The leather of the straps was short but the muscle for pulling was there. Few old buildings remained. New or rebuilt structures stood out everywhere, mainly in a public architecture style. Recovering from World War II, which had destroyed a fifth of its buildings, the city looked like a boomtown. Few buildings of Turkish architecture had survived. Several projects remained unfinished for lack of materials. We saw many long lines of people in front of stores for all kind of goods.

From Belgrade we drove north to an excellent highway. The little traffic consisted mainly of large trucks.

Flooded fields of corn, rye, cabbage and tobacco stretched from either side of the highway. The drive was first through flat and fertile country, past vineyards, brick houses and villages that seemed more prosperous than those in the south. Later we passed through a gently rolling landscape of fields, haystacks and woods. At times, black or spotted cows grazed in the meadows.

There were few hotels outside the major cities, and since we were on a budget we usually camped while in Yugoslavia. It was dark when we stopped for the night in a remote field. My companions made themselves comfortable in the car while I put my sleeping bag right next to the car because I wanted to stretch out after sitting all day.

Suddenly I awoke to a strange noise. Being very sleepy, I opened my eyes reluctantly. To my horror, above me were four soldiers, pointing their guns at me. My first reaction was to jump up, but I couldn't since on each side of my body were the guns. In the darkness I could not see the men's faces. Only the guns and the khaki uniforms of the soldiers were visible. I was frightened when one of the soldiers started to talk to me in Croatian. Then he noticed the Swiss license plates of the car and questioned me in German, which was widely spoken in Croatia.

"What are you doing here?"

"I am traveling through Yugoslavia on my way to Italy," I said.

"When did you come here and when do you plan to leave?"

"We just came to sleep here, and my companions are in the car, they can give you all the necessary information." I was trying to get their attention away from me and go to the car, as it was extremely scary and uncomfortable to talk while lying down with guns facing me. But they did not move and continued the conversation.

"Where are you coming from?"

"We came from Belgrade and Skopje."

"You are in a military camp, and you better get out of here immediately," they responded.

"Yes, we will. I am sorry that we didn't realize we were sleeping in a military field, since it was dark when we camped. Of course, we will leave right away."

To my relief, the soldiers left. I got up and woke Hans and Paul, who had slept through the entire ordeal. I told them what had occurred. We packed up quickly and moved on.

We passed through Zagreb, now the capital of Croatia. There were some stately 19th century buildings, and one could feel the energy of this city. The next brief stop was Ljubljana, the capital of Slovenia. It was a university town that had also become an industrial center. A few modern plants were visible, surrounded by new apartments, schools, stores and theaters.

A side trip took us to Opatja on the Adriatic, not far from Trieste. This picturesque town had been part of Italy with the name of Abbazzia. It used to be a fashionable seaside resort and still had an international atmosphere. French, Italians, English, Germans and Americans mingled on the promenades and beaches with a few Yugoslavs. Former residences of the wealthy had become hotels. The stunning coast, clear waters and many parks had attracted the many tourists. Limestone cliffs seemed to tumble into the sea. The hilltops with pine trees were dotted with ash-gray and terracotta villages and a few castles. We found a deserted beach where we slept and swam the next morning.

We drove the hairpin curves of the coast to Trieste, Italy. This was the end of the car journey from India for me. I left Hans and Paul in Venice, and they continued on to Switzerland. I toured northern Italy by myself for several days before embarking to Israel to visit relatives and work on a Kibbutz.

Turkish woman in Eastern Turkey

Macedonian women in Skopje

Yugoslav Peasants

Yugoslav dancers in a village near Nish

THE ITALIAN BOAT

"Tomorrow we will arrive in beautiful Naples," said the second officer of the Italian steamer *Grimaldi*. I had visited Northern Italy after my trip by car from India and had booked a passage from Genoa to Haifa, Israel to visit my relatives and get to know the country. I had met the second officer as soon as I had embarked and settled in tourist class. He invited me to come to a dance in first class that evening.

I unpacked my one good outfit, a colorful Italian jersey silk dress which I had bought in Milan. An Italian friend invited me to a performance of "La Traviata" at the famous La Scala. I had met him while swimming far out on Lake Como where we started a conversation.

When I arrived at the opera in my new flowered dress, I noticed that all the other women were dressed in black. I looked like the only flower in a sea of black lava and felt very embarrassed.

This time on the dance floor of the *Grimaldi's* first class the dress seemed appropriate. About 50 couples were dancing in the spacious dance hall to soft music. The floor was beautifully polished, and the large chandeliers lightened the room.

"I want to see as much of Naples as I can," I said when finishing the dance with the second officer, a short man in his 30s with slightly curly black hair and a wide mouth that smiled readily. "When do we embark from Naples again?" I asked.

"The *Grimaldi* leaves Naples at noon," he answered.

The next morning we arrived at 8:00 in the port, and

together with my two young cabin companions we
decided to see Naples. We disembarked quickly, without
looking at the bulletin board for announcements as we
were so anxious to take advantage of the limited time.

Both my new friends were Turkish girls who, like me,
had never been to Naples. We hired a horse and buggy
and for the next three and a half hours traveled all over
the city, enjoying every minute of it. We passed the
Castel Nuovo, a massive fortress of the 12th century, the
Royal Palace of the 16th century, the Cathedral and
various other sites and charming piazzas.

Shortly before noon we returned to the pier where
the *Grimaldi* had been anchored. To our horror there
was no *Grimaldi*. The shock was tremendous. We couldn't
believe that the ship had sailed without us. Our luggage,
our passports, our tickets, everything was on board. I
looked toward the sea. There, in the distance, I saw her.
What were we going to do? As the leader of this
expedition, I panicked.

Then I spotted a small U.S. Navy boat at the same
pier.

"I am an American, there is our ship, you must take
us to it right away," I shouted.

"OK, jump in," said one of the sailors quite surprised.
The three of us boarded the little boat and in less than
15 minutes we reached our ship. The sailors had signaled
the *Grimaldi* that three passengers were on their way and
asked her to stop the engines and wait for us.

When we arrived, all the passengers and crew were
lined up on deck to watch the three young women from
tourist class climb up the gangway. Nobody smiled. All

looked indignant, and of course, we were embarrassed and ashamed.

Once in my cabin, the steward came to tell me that the captain wanted to see me. I was terribly worried, as I had heard that the cost for stopping the ship at sea was more than $100, which was a very large sum at that time. I was petrified. There was no way that I could have paid such a fine, as I was the obvious ringleader of the expedition in Naples.

I decided to take the offensive when facing the captain. I put on a nice dress and tried to muster my courage as I proceeded to his cabin at the appointed hour. The gray-haired, saintly-looking man whom I had not met before looked quite stern. Before he could scold me I said: "Sir, don't you wait for your passengers in Italy?"

"Young lady," he responded, "do the trains in the United States wait for passengers that are late?"

"Yes, of course." I figured he had not been in America.

He did not believe me, but he let me go without charging me the fine.

"Neither you nor your two companions may leave the *Grimaldi* at our next stop in Athens. You will have to stay on board until we arrive in Haifa."

By the time we arrived in Athens, everybody had forgotten my punishment. I left the boat and went sightseeing. But I looked twice at the bulletin board that indicated the time of departure from Athens. Long before the appointed hour I safely returned to the *Grimaldi* and prepared for our final destination across the Mediterranean, Haifa.

VIETNAM
1957-1959

After working on a Kibbutz and visiting relatives in Israel, as well as traveling in France and Sweden, I returned to California, where my parents were happy that I had returned safely. For a year I worked as social science librarian at San Francisco State College and then joined a research project on South Asia at the University of California, Berkeley. We wrote handbooks on India, Pakistan and Nepal. My next position was in the Research and Development Division of the Asia Foundation, until I went to Vietnam.

ESTABLISHING A UNIVERSITY LIBRARY AT HUE

The year was 1957, and I was assigned to Vietnam by the Asia Foundation as the library advisor to a new university established in Hue. The Asia Foundation was a private non-governmental organization giving assistance to cultural and educational projects in Asia.

Hue was an ancient city about midway between Hanoi in the north and Saigon (now Ho Chi Minh City) in the south. Hue had been the capital of Imperial Vietnam, and its Old City contained palaces, temples and monuments, some of which were over three hundred years old. Of great importance to scholars, both present and future, were the Imperial Archives, a treasure housed in the Old City.

I lived in the only hotel in town, an old one built by the French, close to the Perfumed River, a name not necessarily apt for the somewhat-polluted waterway that flows through Hue. From my room's balcony I could watch the sampans plying their wares up and down the river, a colorful sight of fruits, vegetables and flowers. My room and all the rooms in the hotel were spacious but dark, gloomy and without heat, as the former colonial style dictated.

I biked daily to the university, where I began my work only to find that there were no restaurants or outdoor food stalls where I could get a meal. Being hungry enough to eat a water buffalo, I found a twelve-man American Advisory Group that was staying at my hotel who readily agreed to let me eat with them at their mess hall at the hotel. In time, I found that the Americans had installed some modern comforts in their part of the hotel, and I obtained the luxury of using the hot water facilities in the commanding officer's quarters at prearranged times.

Life in Hue moved at a slow pace, having none of Saigon's nightlife, movies or good restaurants. Hue was a very conservative town. My work was to help advise Mr. Bu Ke, a well-known poet in his mid-fifties, on the organization and operation of the newly established University of Hue Library. As a literary figure, he loved and admired books, but he had absolutely no experience with cataloguing, classifying or organizing books, all necessary for a library. In fact, in all of South Vietnam (in 1954, after the French defeat at Dien Bien Phu, the subsequent Geneva Convention divided Vietnam into two countries, North and South Vietnam), there were only a handful of librarians who had been trained by the French. A poet was considered an intellectual. Therefore the Vietnamese authorities thought he would be an ideal candidate to fill the role of a university librarian. Mr. Bu Ke was indeed extremely intelligent and thoroughly willing to learn the workings of a modern library from a young foreign woman, even though the conservative dictates of Hue at the time could not conceive of such a breach of etiquette.

There were boxes containing thousands of books in French, English and Vietnamese, most of them donated by France, Canada, Britain and the United States, which Mr. Bu Ke and I worked together to transform into a library useful to university students and faculty. We had a small amount of money, and our staff consisted of one clerk who could type and shelve books. I was anxious to make a meaningful contribution to this effort and could see my few months being wasted unless we could get additional help to type catalogue cards and perform other clerical duties. I wanted to train Mr. Ke to continue the work after I left. The final straw was our complete inability to lay hands on the most basic supplies, such as paper and scotch tape.

I was frustrated and tried all kinds of persuasion with Father Luan, rector (or president) of the university, who had originally asked the Asia Foundation for my help. He listened most politely to my litany of wants, ending our conversation with promises and vagueness. Finally, in desperation I said, "Father Luan, Mr. Ke must have additional help. Our work is not progressing as it should. The University of Saigon has asked for my help with their library, and I probably could make a meaningful contribution there."

"I will get you help," responded the rector, very much alarmed.

Two days later there appeared a new typist/clerk, a young good-looking Vietnamese man with an intelligent face and aristocratic features. He was short, with black hair cropped close and penetrating black eyes. He was in his 30s or early 40s, dressed in a clean pair of light khaki pants and a simple brown sweater, unlike most Vietnamese professionals who usually wore dark suits and ties. I greeted him in French (the second language in Vietnam), and he responded with a warm smile telling me how happy he was to be there, ready to serve Mr. Bu Ke and me. It was no wonder that this man was so happy to be with us in our disorganized new library-to-be. He was an important political prisoner, Nguyen-Van-Ly, formerly Chief of Staff to the Dai Viet Party. That party opposed the regime of Diem, South Vietnam's leader/ dictator supported by the U.S. in the 1950s. The party was anti-communist but backed the former emperor of Vietnam, Bao Dai.

Nguyen-Van-Ly had been a prisoner in Hue for three years and had spent the first two months in solitary confinement. Now he had a taste of limited freedom by coming to the library every day, even though on each visit a prison guard accompanied him. While in prison, he taught himself Japanese and some English. He wanted to take advantage of my presence to learn more English. I taught him for an hour each day, which left the rest of the time for library work. He was not a particularly good typist but applied himself diligently and improved fast. He was always sitting straight in his chair, concentrating on typing catalogue cards. From time to time he looked up and a smile flashed across his face.

Mr. Ly was very interested in learning more about the United States, and as his English improved, he had many questions.

"Is the President elected?" he asked curiously.

"Yes," I answered.

"For how many years?" he queried me.

I then explained the election process.

"Are all the people allowed to vote?" he asked.

"Most are allowed to vote, but unfortunately a large percentage of people who have the right to vote don't," I said.

"Can African-Americans vote?"

He was amazed when I answered affirmatively.

"Oh," he responded. "I thought that they are treated like the untouchables in India."

The English lessons included several chats along these lines. However, I hesitated to discuss Vietnamese politics, because I feared that the dictatorial Diem regime would give me trouble. I hoped we would have the opportunity to explore the questions I had for him in more private surroundings, since Mr. Bu Ke had made it clear that I must be very careful about talking politics with anyone, whether they agreed or not with the present regime.

Our work proceeded more quickly and more smoothly with our new typist. Then Mr. Bu Ke and I decided to change the process of cataloguing to increase speed. After repeated explanations of why we needed to make the changes, we got nowhere with Mr. Ly.

"Ms. Heyman," said Mr. Bu Ke with a smile of resignation, "generals don't take orders."

My only chance to speak with Mr. Ly in private also ended in defeat. I was one of only two or three American women in Hue, and I had paid my respects to the provincial governor's wife as was customary. After this visit, I received a call from the governor's secretary advising me that the governor's wife wanted to visit me. A date was arranged for me to receive her.

That day arrived and, being very nervous about having such an important person visit me, I raced around tidying the room and making sure that all was in the best order that I could manage. I left the library at lunchtime and told Mr. Bu Ke that I would not return to work until the next day. Before I knew it, the hour had arrived, and I heard a knock at my door. Upon opening it, I was horrified to see General Ly standing in front of me. He had chosen that particular day to come, not knowing that I expected the wife of the man who was probably responsible for his imprisonment.

"Oh Mr. Ly," I heard myself shouting. "Please forgive me. I am really very sick. You must go at once." In desperation, I practically pushed him down the stairs. Mr. Ly looked very disappointed. I thought he wanted to apologize but was so intimidated that he could not produce a word. I raced back to my room, slamming the door. I was breathing hard and just barely managed to calm myself when the expected knock came and the governor's wife entered. It was strictly a courtesy visit, with no particular purpose.

The visit went calmly, with polite conversation flowing between us as though there was nothing awry. Had the lady found that prisoner Ly was in the hotel visiting me, there would have been terrible consequences for him in prison, and I would have been forced to leave the country. I never had another chance to talk to him about the politics in Vietnam that had put him in jail. Since then, I have often wondered what he might have told me.

Later, when I left Hue for Saigon to work with the University there, I sent English and Japanese books to Mr. Ly via the Hue library. That act delayed my leaving Vietnam for a couple of weeks, as government officials refused to give me the necessary exit visa before investigating my contact with one of their prominent political prisoners.

THE ARCHIVES

Hue had been the capital of Imperial Vietnam until after World War II. In my free time I often visited the lovely Old City with its interesting temples and palaces where the Vietnamese emperors had lived and ruled.

One of the buildings contained the Imperial Archives. One day while I was working at the Hue University library, a representative of the Ford Foundation from Saigon called and asked me if I would take a look at the Imperial Archives. The Ford Foundation, he told me, was planning to microfilm the collection, or part of the collection. First, it had to be determined if they contained important manuscripts of interest to future scholars.

As library advisor for Vietnam and the only American person in this part of Vietnam with a background in library and information science, the Ford Foundation wanted me to talk to the archivist.

I scheduled an appointment with the archivist for a visit on the following Thursday. My only form of transportation during my stay in Hue was my bicycle, which I used daily to travel to and from the University. I was planning to use it for this mission.

Mr. Bu Ke had become a good friend, and I always asked his advice on anything related to the country and its culture. When told of my plans he said incredulously, "You plan to go to the Old City on your bicycle?" His dark eyes took on a very worried look.

"Yes, you know I have no access to a car, and besides it isn't very far," I replied.

He looked embarrassed. "You are a woman, you are young, and if you arrive on a bicycle, those old Mandarins over there won't even open the door of the archives."

I was indignant. I could possibly make a small contribution to the country and scholarship by reporting to the Ford Foundation on the state of the arts of the archives. What difference should it make how I would be seen arriving! Those were my first thoughts. But I also realized that Mr. Bu Ke was right. I had become familiar with Vietnamese protocol. To compensate for being a woman and having such limited knowledge of Vietnamese culture I must impress the impoverished Mandarins with my power. A taxi would also not do, since taxis are small and used by everybody.

Reluctantly, after having settled the conflict within myself, I called the American consul in Hue. I explained my mission and asked if he could lend me a black car with a driver. He agreed and was pleased to be of assistance. On Thursday, even though it was hot and humid, I put on my most conservative dark dress.

I was driven to the archives, sitting stiffly in the backseat of the large car. Three old Mandarins with white goatees, dressed in long, black, flowing silk robes and Chinese hats saw me coming and opened the door of the archives. They looked like characters from a Chinese opera.

The driver, dressed in a black uniform, opened the door of the black car with consular license plates. In the eyes of the archivists, I was important and rich. Of course, they were willing to show me the archives. We conversed in French and they answered pleasantly and politely my many questions about the contents and background of the materials. The manuscripts in Chinese, Vietnamese and French dealt with the history of Vietnam over several centuries. Even though I didn't read Chinese or Vietnamese, I realized from our conversation that these were important documents. They contained information about the life of the emperors and the edicts that they proclaimed. Some discussed the different wars and were accounts of battles. This I reported to the Ford Foundation.

Eventually many of the materials were microfilmed. In the late '60s the war destroyed much of the Old City, including the archives. Fortunately, the most important documents had been saved on microfilm. I was pleased to have played a small part in the preservation of at least some of the materials.

THE BIRTHDAY PARTY

It was Father Luan's birthday. He was the rector of the University of Hue, and he invited me to a dinner party. I was honored and accepted the invitation with pleasure.

I sat at one end of the table. About twenty faculty members, all men, attended the dinner. It was not the custom at that time to bring wives. Thus, I was the only woman, as happened often in my travels and work in Asia in the '50s and '60s. It was quite noisy; conversation was in a mixture of Vietnamese and French. The professors on each side of me spoke in French and often translated Vietnamese jokes for me. I didn't feel very comfortable but just smiled when the others laughed.

The party consisted of a ten-course dinner with a mixture of French and Vietnamese food. There was beer and wine, and everybody enjoyed the food and drinks. One dish was some meat in a delicious French sauce. It was a little tough, but I always ate everything at Vietnamese parties in order not to offend my hosts.

The next day one of the professors, who had studied in England, came to me and asked, "How did you enjoy the party last night?"

"I enjoyed it very much," I replied.

"Do you know what you ate?" he continued with a malicious smile.

"No, but everything was good," I answered politely and honestly.

"Well, the meat was dog, which we consider a delicacy, only served on special occasions."

I was shocked but didn't want to show it. I was wondering if I would have eaten the main dish if I had known its contents. Probably not, but it was too late to worry about it.

SQUARE DANCING IN HUE

"What can we do for our students?" said Dr. Hoan, an economics professor who had often come to the library. He had studied in France and the United States. "Isn't there some activity, something that you could suggest other than studies, reading and courses, that the students would enjoy in their free time, like in the United States?"

I thought for a few minutes. "What about folk dancing or square dancing? Do you think they would be interested?"

"That would be great. Can you help start a square dance group?"

I had never taught folk dancing or square dancing, though I had done it in the past. The idea intrigued me, and I thought it would be a lot of fun to form a square dance group for these nice Vietnamese students, who had no extra-curricular programs at the University.

I called the American Consul in Hue and asked if he could help. He said he would get some square dance records from the United States Information Agency in Saigon and that he and his wife, the only other American civilians in the town, would be happy to participate.

We put signs in the library and other places around the university inviting the students to come and square dance in the library on a designated day.

The day arrived and we had the records. Dr. Hoan, another professor and his wife who had studied in England, the consul and his wife and I had practiced a few days prior. Now, in addition to our little group, seven students—four girls and three boys—showed up in the library where we had cleared some space among the books and tables.

The music started. John, the consul, shouted out the instructions along with the records. The girls wore their *ao dais*, the flowing Vietnamese dress, and the boys wore clean white shirts and slacks. First, they were hesitant, but soon they were smiling. After half an hour there was even laughter and shouts of enjoyment. All tried the different steps with varied success.

When we finished our first session, by all accounts a success, we told them that we would do this every Friday and that they should bring their friends.

The next Friday, our core group was joined by eleven additional Vietnamese students. We were encouraged. In this second session the students' steps were more regular, though there was some confusion as to how to turn and change partners which generated much laughter. We thought we had given the students some pleasant recreation in this quiet conservative town.

Three days later Dr. Hoan came to see me. "We have to stop the dancing. The governor heard that boys and girls are holding hands while square dancing." This was too progressive in the repressive, conservative atmosphere of Hue in the 1950s.

Juliane in a Vietnamese dress (ao dai)

Juliane, Mr. Bu Ke the librarian and clerk at
the Hue University Library

Father Luan, Rector of the University with
faculty members and Juliane at a meeting at
the University of Hue

The library of the University of Hue

PAKISTAN

When I returned from Vietnam, I became Pakistan Program Officer at the Asia Foundation. In 1961 Michigan State University called and offered me a job as library consultant to the two Pakistan Academies for Village Development, one in Comilla, East Pakistan (now Bangladesh) and one in Peshawar. As I had developed a special interest for South Asia, I was happy to accept. When President Kennedy in his inauguration speech said: "Ask not what your country can do for you, but what you can do for your country," I felt that I was doing something worthwhile for my country.

KAGHAN VALLEY ADVENTURE

"Why don't you come to tea at our lodge, just a few miles from here," said the saintly-looking Pakistani colonel in his early 60s to Aquilla and me. "You will also be able to fish."

My friend Aquilla, who had a Ph.D from Columbia University, was very much respected by all our male colleagues at the Academy. She was a small woman with dark eyes and long black hair. At work she always wore a beautiful sari, but for this excursion she wore slacks and a sweater. Her husband, a pilot with Pakistan Airlines, was often abroad, and her two young sons were with her mother. We had decided to take this trip together. She wanted to show me the splendor of the Karakoram mountain range, which includes K2, the second-highest peak in the world.

We were in the mountains in the northwestern part of Pakistan, on vacation for a few days from our work at the Academy of Village Development in Peshawar. After a rough ten-hour Jeep trip on narrow mountain roads, we had arrived at Lake Saiful Muluk. The turquoise lake was flanked by glaciers. It was afternoon, and the sun's rays were falling on the gently rippling water.

While taking a little rest from the long trip, we had met the colonel and five young men in army uniforms. They were also enjoying the tranquil scenery.

It was 1961 and few tourists were visiting this remote part of Pakistan. The officers were surprised to meet two young women, one Pakistani and one American, without a male chaperon. When they learned where we were from, they seemed pleased to meet ladies from academia and invited us to their lodge.

"We would be delighted to come to tea," I said.

"Very well, follow our Jeep to the lodge where we will welcome you," answered the colonel.

Having tea after traveling all day on dusty roads and trails sounded inviting, as did the offer to do some fishing. Aquilla hesitated. It was not customary for a young Pakistani lady to visit an army camp. Silently she nodded, which meant she agreed when she realized how excited I was to go fishing.

The driver of our Jeep followed the officer's Jeep to the guesthouse. It was a rustic two-story lodge made of wood. The living room was spacious but sparsely furnished. About twenty officers of all ranks and ages welcomed us. They ranged in age from early 20s to 60s. The officers had gathered at this lodge to bid farewell to the colonel, who was about to retire. We had tea, exchanged pleasantries and then went fishing. They provided us with first-class fishing gear, but the local fishermen at the stream with ordinary bamboo rods and old lines had better luck than us. They caught fish after fish. It was a windy afternoon, and the weather was blamed for our failure to catch fish. A poor fisherman gave Aquilla two of his catches. We rewarded him with some rupees, which he gladly accepted.

Before our departure, we returned to the lodge where one young captain said, "We would like to have a picture of your visit with us."

We obliged and the officer photographed the group, the two of us surrounded by twenty army officers. We said goodbye and continued our journey. When we were alone, Aquilla seemed upset.

"One of the officers is from my husband's village," she said. "If my husband's family sees the picture, it will be embarrassing to my husband."

Even though she always worked with men as an equal and was completely accepted professionally, to have tea with twenty army men was not socially accepted at the time.

I didn't want to create any problems for my friend, particularly since I had been eager to visit the lodge. What to do?

We decided that I would have to lure the photographer into giving me the group's picture before it could be seen by anybody in the village of her husband's family.

Before leaving our new friends, we had exchanged addresses. The officers had implied that they would visit us in Peshawar. After a week, I called the captain and invited him and the others to have tea at my house in Peshawar.

"I am anxious to see the photo you took. It will be a lovely memory of our mountain excursion."

A few days later he came with three others and brought the picture.

"Please give me not only the print but also the negative. I want to make some copies for my entire family in the United States," I said.

He was surprised, but as a gentleman he could not refuse my request. I never returned the negative to its owner and never saw the captain again.

Juliane and Aquilla Kiani in the
Kaghan Valley

Our jeep going over a glacier in the
Kaghan Valley

Juliane teaching library science in Pakistan

NEPAL

While I was in Pakistan, Sargent Shriver, director of the newly established Peace Corps, visited the Academy of Village Development in Comilla in East Pakistan, because its director was one of the first persons who had introduced the concept of community development. His visits were followed by some of his staff with whom I had long discussions. I thought that I would like to work for the Peace Corps when I finished my contract in Pakistan, and that is what I did from 1961 to 1966. As training officer, and later as Deputy of the Near East/ South Asia Division of the Training Department, I was responsible for designing and administering training programs for volunteers. During these years I traveled extensively to universities all over the country and made trips to Thailand, India and Nepal.

WITHOUT A BACKPACK

It was my second trip to Nepal. I visited the country in 1958 while working in Vietnam. In 1964, I returned to escort a group of new volunteers, but the main purpose of the trip was to evaluate our training programs.

The change that I noticed immediately upon my arrival in Kathmandu was the number of cars. In 1958 there was only one car in the capital, now there were perhaps three or four dozen jeeps and cars, most of them belonging to foreign assistance groups. A few more hotels had been built to accommodate the increasing number of tourists.

I stayed with Willie Unsoeld, the Peace Corps director in Nepal, whom I had known when we worked together during training programs. Willie, a member of the first American Everest Expedition, had made the ascent of Everest the year before. A few years later, I had the privilege of climbing with him in the Tetons. In the 1980s he was killed while climbing Mt. Rainier in Washington State.

After visits with volunteers in the Kathmandu Valley and Gorkha, which I had reached by plane, Willie and I participated in a conference for community development volunteers in the Terai, in the South of the country. All of the young men—there were no women in this group—had been my trainees.

The Terai is a narrow strip of flat and fertile land wedged between the Indian border and the mountains. At the time much of the land was forested and it was home to many wild animals. We had taken a jeep to travel to the Terai, but once there, we took an elephant ride. The climate was very humid, hot and sticky. Therefore many of us slept on the roof of the government building where the conference took place. Once or twice during the night, I got up to go under the pump in the yard, because when the skirt and blouse that I was wearing were wet, it cooled my body for a short time.

After the conference, I decided to go to Dankhuta, a small town in Eastern Nepal where a number of volunteers were living. John Franklin, a volunteer who had to return to Dankhuta, accompanied me, We took a jeep to Dharan and from there trekked for two days.

A sherpa carried my little suitcase, while John had a backpack. I was wearing a skirt and blouse, as it was not common for women in Nepal to wear pants at that time. We also carried umbrellas for the sun and rain.

The trails were narrow paths running between rice paddies and fields. They were primarily paths that were the result of people having walked over the same route for generations. We had many ascents and descents. The trip led us from one valley to the next, past farms, villages, through forests and across several sharp ridges. There was nothing monotonous about going up and down the hills as there were different views around almost every corner of the winding track. Most spectacular were the vistas of the snow-covered Himalayas in the distance.

Along the trail we met many sturdy and gay Nepalis carrying heavy burdens of wood and large baskets filled with different items. They always greeted us with a friendly "namaste." We did not see any Westerners, as trekking in Nepal only became popular a few years later.

In the evening we stopped at a tea house. Before we spread our sleeping bags on the mud floor of the simple hut, we joined the Nepali men around the open fire to have tea and "daal bhaat," a dish of rice and lentils.

John, who spoke Nepali, conversed with the men. I only knew a dozen words of the language which I had picked up while visiting the training programs. When they asked us where we were from, and John answered from America, they shook their heads as they had never heard of America. Distances to them were only real in terms of trekking days. We figured that Nepal was roughly 20,000 km from New York. Then we calculated that Nepalis could walk perhaps up to 30 km. a day and told them it might take about two years to trek to our country. We explained that there was a large ocean and we had not trekked but had come by plane.

The next morning we continued our journey to Dhankuta, which we reached in the afternoon. Dhankuta was an attractive hill town surrounded by forests and with splendid views of the Himalayas from some spots. It had pleasant white-washed houses and winding streets paved with stones.

I stayed with volunteers for four days, getting a lot of feedback which would be useful to improve future training programs. Most of them were teachers, so I attended their classes and otherwise participated in the activities of the town.

John, who remained in Dhankuta, arranged for a sherpa who also could guide me to Biratnagar from where I could take a plane to Kathmandu. In order to reach Dharan in one day, from where I could continue by bus, I left very early in the morning, only accompanied by the sherpa with whom I could hardly converse. Nevertheless, I enjoyed the return trip as much as I had the trekking to Dhankuta.

When I arrived at the airport in Biratnagar, I learned that all four or five planes of the Royal Nepal Airlines had been commandeered to West Nepal to bring rice to that region. No one could tell me when flights to Kathmandu would resume.

I wondered what I should do. There was no way I could communicate with Willie Unsoeld in Kathmandu. I didn't think there were any suitable hotels in the town. I remembered that the former Nepali ambassador to the United States, whom I had met in Washington, was living in Biratnagar.

I told the rickshaw driver to take me to Ambassador Koirala's house. The Koiralas were a well known family in Nepal, one having served as Prime Minister in 1959. Without knowing the address, the rickshaw took me to the Ambassador's house.

"Ms. Heyman, you brought your suitcase," said the Ambassador when he came to the door and saw me in the rickshaw. I didn't know if he was surprised that I did not carry a backpack or that he realized I needed accommodations.

After I explained my dilemma, he invited me to stay with him and was a most gracious host. For the next three days, he drove me every day to the airport to check whether any planes were available for the flight to Kathmandu. Then I decided I could no longer wait in Biratnagar because I had to return to the U.S. to begin new training programs. I took a bus to the Indian border, and traveled through northern India by train on a narrow-gauge track which seemed to take forever. Finally I arrived at the Nepali frontier from where I could take a truck. The ninety-mile Tribbuvan Rajpath, built in the 1950s by Indian engineers, was the only completed motor-road at the time. After some hours in the Terai, the road climbed over mountains, crossing a pass of more than 8,000 feet. Mountains were on all sides of the valleys we crossed, and the slopes and crests were heavily wooded and freshly green. The truck toiled around many hairpin bends and at times reminded me of my trip through Afghanistan.

More than two days after I left Biratnagar I arrived in Kathmandu. Willie Unsoeld had not worried about me, as he was confident that I would manage to return. With almost no existing communication facilities in the country, he was used to not hearing from persons traveling in Nepal.

Two days later I was able to get a flight to the U.S., a delay in my original plans.

Juliane with Peace Corps Volunteers in the Terai

John Franklin, Peace Corps Volunteer who
was my trekking companion to Dhankuta

School children in Dhankuta

EL SALVADOR

After my years in the Peace Corps, I took a long vacation in Spain, France and Yugoslavia before returning to Washington to work with non-profit organizations on international development projects financed by the Agency for International Development. In 1969 I received a contract from the A.I.D. for El Salvador.

THE SOCCER WAR

"There will be no war," said the American Ambassador to El Salvador. This was the response to Mark, my new boss, the deputy director of A.I.D.

"War, what are they talking about?" I thought. It was 1969, and I had arrived in San Salvador the previous day to start working with the educational television team. My friend Henning had helped me drive my car from Washington to San Salvador from where he returned to his job in Washington by air. It had taken us two weeks during which we crossed Mexico and Guatemala. In the south of Mexico we had put the car on a train for a stretch, as the Pan American Highway had not yet been completed. We had not seen any news or read a paper for a week.

Mark came to welcome me that day at the Intercontinental Hotel in San Salvador "I will present

you to the Ambassador," he said. I was surprised. I, a
mere consultant, was wondering why I would meet the
Ambassador so soon.

At our meeting in the spacious, well-decorated
office, it soon became clear to me that Mark was using
the official presentation to learn more about the political
situation. He only gave the Ambassador my name and
mentioned briefly what I was going to do. There were
no further questions from the Ambassador, and the talk
was about a possible confrontation between El Salvador
and Honduras. I sat there, wondering what all this was
about.

Unconcerned I returned to the hotel. I spent my time
thinking about the next day, when I was going to San
Andres to meet the Americans and El Salvadorians with
whom I was going to work.

I retired early that night, at about 10:00 p.m. I was
awakened by the "boom, boom, boom" of low-flying
planes and bombs. The phone rang and the receptionist
told me to go into the hall immediately. Dressed in my
robe, I went into the hall, and saw in front of every door
the other hotel guests. "No war" I had been assured by
the Ambassador a few hours before. What was this? I
certainly was acquainted with the roar of bombs, having
lived in Europe during World War II.

During the next few hours I learned from the other
guests that Honduras had attacked El Salvador, or vice
versa. The Honduras Air Force only had planes that were
used for crop-dusting and therefore were not very
accurate. Fortunately bombs did not hit the hotel
directly.

At about 1:00 a.m. the bombing stopped and we were allowed to go back to our rooms. Mark called to tell me that there was a war, and that I had to stay at the hotel till further notice.

The next day the hotel emptied. By the third day, every guest—except for me and an English professor who was also a consultant to AID—had departed. We listened to the radio, read newspapers, went swimming and kept ourselves busy with rumors, gossip and tales of war. I was not too worried, although I was bored and frustrated that I could not start my work.

This was what was known as the "soccer war." It had started when Honduras and El Salvador played the World Cup in San Salvador, which ended in fights among the fans from each team. The real cause of the war, however, was social inequity and overpopulation in El Salvador. Lack of land and poverty forced many Salvadorians to immigrate to Honduras, a larger country with a smaller population. But recently the Honduras government had expelled them. This created even greater problems for El Salvador, which had to absorb these poor, landless refugees. It was probably the first population war. The result was the resurrection of the military and the beginning of the many years of civil war that followed.

The war, which lasted five days, was won by El Salvador. I was not allowed to leave the hotel for nine days, as A.I.D. wanted to make sure that everything was quiet and normal before we could go back to work. Thus, I spent almost two weeks of my stay in El Salvador in a hotel. After that, everything returned to normalcy.

I was quite amused when I saw signs in San Salvador, "Moshe, we did it in five days," referring to Moshe Dayan of Israel who had defeated the Arab countries in the six-day war two years earlier.

EPILOGUE

After my return to Washington from El Salvador, I felt I needed a change from the politics of Washington for a year and went to Aspen, Colorado. I stayed three years, however, teaching languages and history at the Aspen Country Day School as well as the Colorado Mountain College. I fell in love with Aspen.

I worked also intermittently for the Aspen Institute helping with conferences and research for a seminar on "Basic Human Needs." I was well suited for such research because of my background and experience.

In my free time I enjoyed hiking and climbing, including many of Colorado's 14,000 foot mountains, as well as skiing downhill and cross country in winter. In addition, I participated in many seminars offered by the Aspen Institute and attended the marvelous concerts of the Aspen Music Festival. For me it was a happy time.

After three years,however, I felt the need to return to my career in Washington. I rented out the house which I had acquired while living in Aspen and settled down in an apartment. I immediately helped with the unsuccessful Presidential campaign of Sargent Shriver for a few weeks. After that I worked on several international development projects for different consultant firms and non-profit organizations. These projects dealt with international population education and family planning in the Caribbean and Central America.

Twice I traveled to Mauritania in Africa. The climate there and the numerous sandstorms were difficult to cope with. Nevertheless I was content to work in and learn about another culture. My job entailed setting up a database, which allowed me to do research in other African countries and Europe.

After several years I returned to California and settled in Santa Barbara. There I continued a few short-term consultant jobs and taught current events for the Adult Education program of Santa Barbara City College.

At this time I divide my time between Santa Barbara and Aspen, two very beautiful places. I continue to travel and explore, always in search of new knowledge.

This book represents only a few stories of my interesting and rich life that are meant to give a view of a world that no longer exists. Most of the countries that I visited in the 1950s and 1960s unfortunately have become known mostly for their most recent hostilities or political turmoil.

I have always been ready to face many challenges, whether physical, emotional or intellectual. I have never sought out special treatment as a woman, but always felt like one. My experiences have given me new depth and understanding of different people and I hope I have touched the lives of some.

BVG